MW00651153

# METHODISTS
# IN
# MECKLENBURG

*A History of the*
*United Methodist Church*
*In Mecklenburg County*

by Russell Ford

© 2004 Russell W. Ford, Jr.

All Rights Reserved

Library of Congress Control Number: 2004094404

ISBN: 0-9759530-2-8

Printed in the USA by
JOSTENS, Charlotte, N. C.

Russell W. Ford, Jr.
9630 Watergate Road
Charlotte, NC 28270-2106

# CONTENTS

*Every state of society owes much of its character for excellence or demerit, to the generations that preceded; the present is a reflected image of the past; and men must search among their ancestors for the principles, and causes, and springs of action, and moulding influences, that have made society and themselves what they are.*

The Rev. William Henry Foote, 1846

# 1

# "The First Rise of Methodism"

Compared to other religious bodies, Methodism is a young denomination. When the first settlers came to Mecklenburg County, most of them were Presbyterians. A few were Lutherans. But none were members of the Methodist Church, for one simple reason: There was no such thing as The Methodist Church.

In fact, Mecklenburg County and Methodism came into being, developed and flourished almost simultaneously. Consider the following sequence of events, all occurring within the span of a half century:

| | |
|---|---|
| 1735 | John and Charles Wesley go to Georgia as missionaries |
| 1738 | John Wesley's transforming experience at Aldersgate |
| 1740 | (approximately) First settlers in Mecklenburg County area |
| 1744 | Wesley organizes first Methodist conference in England |
| 1760 | (approximately) Robert Strawbridge preaches in Maryland |
| 1762 | Mecklenburg County created |
| 1767 | Francis Asbury accepted into Wesleyan connection |
| 1767 | Lord Selwyn sells 360 acres for town of Charlotte |
| 1768 | Charlotte receives town charter |
| 1772 | Joseph Pilmoor—first Methodist missionary to N.C. |
| 1773 | First Methodist conference in Philadelphia |
| 1775 | Mecklenburg Declaration of Independence |
| 1784 | Methodist Episcopal Church organized in Baltimore |
| 1785 | Origin of Harrison's, Mecklenburg's first Methodist church |

Many of the Methodists in early Mecklenburg, perhaps even most, were converted from other traditions, or from no committed religion at all. Some were people who had become disaffected with existing denominations. Some had allowed their faith to slide because their isolation had deprived them of opportunities to join in fellowship with other believers. Some were too poor to afford the means to travel the miles to one of those early Presbyterian churches. Perhaps the rigors of frontier life had simply focused their attention and energy on other concerns.

But their souls hungered for spiritual nourishment. They were drawn to camp meetings and listened as visiting evangelists thundered the gospel message. Wesley's views on free grace—essentially that everyone has a chance to be saved—and the Methodist style of heartfelt, off-the-cuff preaching warmed their hearts and stirred their spirits. They began to form groups known as societies which, over time, became churches.

The term Methodist actually goes back many years before John and Charles Wesley. There are records of people being called "Methodists" as much as two centuries before the Wesleyan movement began.

The first use of the term may have referred to a group of physicians who believed that all illness could be treated through a particular "method" of diet or lifestyle. Later, the term was used scornfully for people who seemed overly serious, or "methodical," in their worship.

Today, we tend to associate the name "Methodist" exclusively with the followers of John Wesley, and the churches they organized. However, this was not always the case. For example, in Great Britain there is a group known as "Calvinistic Methodists" who are actually Presbyterian in their beliefs. The eighteenth century evangelist George Whitefield is usually called a Methodist. It is no surprise that Methodists would like to claim Whitefield. He was surely one of the most popular and most influential evangelists ever to preach in America. Yet, the only time he had what could be considered a working relationship with Wesley was during and immediately following their college years in England.[1] Numerous others came to be called "Methodists;" some because they, like Wesley, were leading reform movements within the Church of England; and some because their manner of preaching or religious philosophy reminded observers of Wesley. A few had been associated with the Holy Club at Oxford; others had no ties at all to the Wesleyan movement. In 18th and 19th century America, it appears from some writings that the label *Methodist* was rather loosely applied to almost any traveling evangelist, regardless of his affiliation.

At times the manner and behavior of persons incorrectly labeled as Methodists brought undeserved rebuke on Wesley's movement. Wesley commented on this in a letter to an Anglican clergyman:

> ...that title of reproach, *Methodist*, is now affixed to many people who are not under my care, nor ever had any connexion with me. And what have I to do with these? If you give me a nickname and then give it to others whom I know not, does this make me accountable for them? either for their principles or practice? In nowise. I am to answer [only] for myself, and for those that are in connexion with me."[2]

Although United Methodists today are universally regarded as Protestants, the denomination, strictly speaking, was not a direct product of the Protestant Reformation.[3]

The Reformation began on October 31, 1517, when Martin Luther nailed his famous 95 theses to the church door in Wittenberg, Germany. In 1532 John Calvin, a French theologian, launched a reform movement of his own, leading to that great body of churches we know today as Presbyterian. John Knox would carry the faith to Scotland, where it became the state church and bedrock belief of the Scots and Scots-Irish, those hardy founders of Charlotte.

The reform movement was gaining attention in England, but the Church of England, from which John Wesley came, was cut off from Rome for an altogether different reason. It was not so much a disagreement over theology when King Henry VIII threw off papal authority and proclaimed himself head of the English church in 1529.

The king just wanted to get a divorce, and the Pope wouldn't allow it. After its separation from Rome, the Anglican Church took its time reshaping itself from its Catholic image. Priests and bishops remained, though no longer under papal authority. Priestly celibacy wasn't abandoned until 1532, when the twice-married Thomas Cranmer was named archbishop of Canterbury. Other traditions of the Roman church fell away gradually. Monasteries were abolished in 1536. The First Book of Common Prayer was published in the English language in 1549.

Two centuries after King Henry rebuffed the Pope, John Wesley launched what became the Methodist movement. Wesley was born at Epworth, England, in 1703, the 15th child of Samuel and Susannah Wesley. He graduated from Oxford University in 1724 and was ordained the following year.

John's younger brother Charles also enrolled at Oxford, where he formed a group which became known as the "Holy Club." At first the club was a social organization, but soon they began to focus intently on their religious lives. When John Wesley returned to Oxford in 1729 as an instructor he became leader of the Holy Club.

Many people, including Wesley himself, look back on the Holy Club as the beginning of Methodism. In some respects, they would be right. First, it popularized the name "Methodist" which Wesley accepted and later applied to his followers. Further, The Holy Club was a prototype for Wesley's future "societies" and "classes," in which believers came together in groups outside the established church to worship, study, and re-examine their religious lives.

And most significantly, the club was an early manifestation of Wesley's personal quest for a better understanding of his own religious faith. He sensed a need for something beyond mere attendance at the ritual formalities of the Established Church. In the Holy Club he sought salvation through even more demanding ritual and sacrificial living. Club members led highly disciplined lives, with time set aside for study, scripture reading, daily devotions, and self examination. They fasted on Wednesdays and Fridays and spent Saturdays preparing for communion and worship on Sundays. They believed

*John Wesley*
*Oil on canvas, painted in Tewksbury, England, by an unknown artist in 1771. Wesley presented it to John Cole, along with a letter of commendation to the Methodists in America. Cole and his family emigrated to America in 1785. Reputed to be the first oil painting of Wesley in the colonies. Wesley was 68 years old in 1771. He was described as small in stature, about five feet three, and weighing about 126 pounds.[4] It was said that his bright hazel eyes had a penetrating quality which remained into old age. A UMNS photo reproduced with permission from the Methodist Collection of Drew University Library.*

that good works were an essential part of their religious life, and spent much time visiting prisons and helping the poor. As Wesley himself later wrote, "The exact regularity of their lives, as well as studies, occasioned a young gentleman of Christ Church to say, 'Here is a new set of Methodists sprung up;' alluding to some ancient physicians who were so called."[5] Wesley would later refer to this as "the first rise of Methodism."[6]

With all due respect to Mr. Wesley, however, today's United Methodist Church bears little resemblance to the Holy Club in beliefs or practices. Not until other events changed the course of their lives did the Wesleys take steps which led to formation of the Methodist Church as we know it today.

In March 1735 John Wesley and his brother Charles sailed to America as missionaries for the Church of England, with a principal aim of bringing Christianity to the Indians and colonists in the backwoods of Georgia. Their journey would prove mostly unfruitful. Within nine months Charles returned to England. John Wesley remained for two more years, preaching to settlers and Indians in Georgia. He established a small religious society while there, meeting once or twice a week for religious instruction and mutual support.[7] But this society was formed within the Anglican congregation of Savannah, and is not generally recognized as the beginning of Methodism in America.

A more meaningful event in the development of Methodism had occurred during the Wesleys' passage to America. Aboard ship the English passengers were terrified by a severe storm, but a group of German Moravians were calmly singing. Wesley asked one later, "Were you not afraid?" The German indicated that faith in God had carried them through.[8]

Back in London, Wesley became friends with a young Moravian, Peter Böhler.[9] The young man had a deep influence on Wesley, and together they formed a group they called the "Fetter Lane Society" based on societies found within the Moravian movement.

***Wesley preaches on his father's tombstone—***
*Because of his innovative style of preaching,*
*Wesley was denied the privilege of speaking inside*
*many churches. On a visit to Epworth, where he*
*was born, Wesley preached a Sunday evening*
*sermon outdoors. He wrote in his journal for*
*Sunday, June 6, 1742, "Accordingly at six I came*
*and found such a congregation as I believe*
*Epworth never saw before. I stood near the east*
*end of the church, upon my father's tombstone,*
*and cried, "The kingdom of heaven is not meat*
*and drink; but righteousness, and peace, and joy*
*in the Holy Ghost" The scene above is from a*
*window (right), which was contributed to*
*Hawthorne Lane United Methodist Church by a*
*charter member, department store founder J. B.*
*Ivey, in memory of his parents, the Rev. George*
*W. and Selina Neal Ivey.*

It was during this time that Wesley began to put shape to his emerging religious convictions, and developed the core beliefs that would energize the future Methodist movement. On May 24, 1738, while attending a service in Aldersgate, Wesley reports he felt his heart "strangely warmed."

Although he would later part ways with the Moravians, the experience would be a turning point in Wesley's spiritual journey. His preaching took on a new power and focus.

John Wesley was a prolific writer. His journal, covering the period 1735 to 1790, fills four volumes. His letters, essays and sermons fill more than a dozen additional volumes. His writing is filled with interesting anecdotes, and even occasionally shows a dry sense of humor. At one place in his journal he describes an encounter with a stranger on horseback while riding to Leicestershire:

> ...I overtook a serious man with whom I immediately fell into conversation. He presently gave me to know what his opinions were; therefore I said nothing to contradict them. But that did not content him. He was quite uneasy to know "whether I held the doctrine of the decrees as he did;" but I told him over and over "We had better keep to practical things lest we should be angry at one another." And so we did for two miles, till he caught me unawares, and dragged me into the dispute before I knew where I was. He then grew warmer and warmer; told me I was rotten at heart and supposed I was one of John Wesley's followers. I told him "No. I am John Wesley himself." Upon which he would gladly have run away outright. But being the better mounted of the two I kept close to his side and endeavored to show him his heart till we came into the street of Northampton.[10]

On another occasion he relates a story of some religious converts being brought before a magistrate:

> I rode over to a neighbouring town, to wait upon a Justice of Peace, a man of candour and understanding; before whom (I was informed) their angry neighbours had carried a whole waggon-load of these new heretics. But when he asked, what they had done? There was a deep silence; for that was a point their conductors had forgot. At length one

said, "Why they pretended to be better than other people. And besides; they prayed from morning to night." Mr. S. asked, "But have they done nothing besides?" "Yes, Sir," said an old man; "An't please your worship, they have converted my wife. Till she went among them she had such a tongue! And now, she is as quiet as a lamb." "Carry them back, carry them back," replied the Justice, "and let them convert all the scolds in the town."[11]

From the start Wesley focused his efforts on those not being served by the Established Church—the impoverished and the working classes. His message of free grace resounded with them, and he attracted crowds of eager listeners. As his preaching attracted followers, Wesley established what he called United Societies, and appointed lay preachers to help spread the word.

While he differed with the Church in some practices, John Wesley remained an Anglican priest all his life. His Methodist "classes" were essentially a collection of Bible study and worship fellowships, and did not become a separate denomination in England until after his death.[12] In 1744 he organized the first Methodist Conference in England. But the movement was destined to spread throughout the world.

## Chapter Notes

1. Although George Whitefield's revivalist preaching helped create the climate in which American Methodism would later develop, he was not a part of the Methodist connection organized and directed by Wesley. Whitefield's identification as a Methodist apparently stems from his membership in Wesley's "Holy Club" at Oxford, and a brief association with Wesley in the earliest days of their work in England, in 1738-39. The two great preachers separated their work entirely in March 1741. Whitefield died in Massachusetts in 1770 and is buried there at a Presbyterian church.
2. John Wesley, *Works,* Vol. 9, p. 101.
3. *The Book of Discipline of the United Methodist Church,* 1972 edition, p. 7.
4. Heitzenrater, Richard, *The Elusive Mr. Wesley,* Vol. 1, p. 21. Other sources say Wesley was slightly taller, as much as five feet six inches.
5. "A short History of Methodism" by John Wesley, one of a series in *John Wesley: Holiness of Heart and Life,* provided on the internet by the United Methodist General Board of Global Ministries. The text may be found at www.gbgm-umc.org/umw/wesley.
6. John Telford, *The Life of John Wesley,* p. 147. Wesley also called his formation of the society in Georgia the "second rise of Methodism" and the Fetter Lane Society as the "third rise of Methodism."
7. John Wesley, *Journal,* April 17, 1736.
8. *Ibid.,* January 25, 1736.
9. Charles Sauer, *A Pocket Story of John Wesley,* p. 21.
10. Wesley, *Journal,* May 20, 1742.
11. *Ibid.,* June 9, 1742.
12. Wesley's position on this was well known. One particular reference to it is found in his journal entry for April 12, 1789: "Afterward I met the society and explained to them at large the original design of the Methodists, namely, not to be a distinct party but to stir up all parties, Christians or heathens, to worship God in spirit and in truth; but the Church of England in particular, to which they belonged from the beginning. With this view I have uniformly gone on for fifty years, never varying from the doctrine of the Church at all; nor from her discipline, of choice, but of necessity; so, in a course of years, necessity was laid upon me (as I have proved elsewhere) 1) to preach in the open air; 2) to pray extempore; 3) to form societies; 4) to accept of the assistance of lay preachers; and, in a few other instances, to use such means as occurred, to prevent or remove evils that we either felt or feared."

# 2

# A New Nation,
# A New Church

There is room for debate about the beginnings of Methodism in America. Some point to a society formed by John Wesley in Savannah, Georgia, in 1736 while he was there as a missionary for the Church of England. Wesley himself would later refer to this as "the second rise of Methodism," the "first rise" being formation of the Holy Club at Oxford seven years earlier. The Savannah group consisted of some 30 or 40 of the "serious members" of his Anglican congregation. They met weekly at Wesley's home for religious instruction, study and prayer. Wesley called it a first rudiment of the Methodist societies. Still, it is plain that Wesley had no intention of forming a new denomination; the idea probably didn't even occur to him. He viewed this group, even as he viewed later Methodist societies in England, as being within the Established Church, formed only for the purpose of enriching and deepening the members' religious experience. In any case, the Savannah society did not survive after Wesley returned to England, and it would be another 70 years before the first permanent Methodist congregation would be organized there.

Another group formed in Lewes, Delaware, in 1739[1] has also been called by some "the first Methodist society in America." This group came together after several visits to the area by evangelist George Whitefield. However, while Whitefield is often called a Methodist, he was neither working for, nor directed by, John Wesley. He was, in essence, a freelance evangelist, and he was more closely aligned to the Presbyterian denomination. In any event, the Lewes society did not long continue, and it remained for a Wesley preacher,

Freeborn Garretson, to initiate a permanent society in Lewes 40 years later.

The first Methodists genuinely associated with Wesley's movement probably arrived on these shores in the 1750s. Wesley had begun forming societies in England around 1740, and the movement soon spread to Ireland and Scotland. Some individual Methodists involved in these groups were likely among immigrants to America in the years soon thereafter.

In 1760 Robert Strawbridge, a farmer from Ireland, began preaching in Maryland, and later in Virginia, Delaware and Pennsylvania. He is credited with planting Methodism in Baltimore, where it quickly grew into one of the movement's most prominent societies.[2] Unlike Whitefield, Strawbridge was a follower of Wesley. Converted under the preaching of Wesley in Ireland, Strawbridge was a gifted lay preacher and skilled as an organizer, but he was not given to working within the system. According to Lee, Strawbridge was admitted on trial as a traveling preacher in 1773, but never entered the full connection.[3]

The group most often recognized as the first permanent Methodist society in America was formed in New York by Philip Embury and his cousin, Barbara Heck, in 1766. Originally the meetings were held in Embury's home, but they soon moved into a rented room nearby, then into an old rigging loft. The congregation grew rapidly, and within two years they had built the first Methodist meeting house in America. Embury preached the dedicatory sermon on October 30, 1768. The meeting house was known as Wesley's Chapel.

Captain Thomas Webb, who had been instrumental in drawing members to the New York society, then began working in Philadelphia. All of these groups functioned without ordained leadership.

In 1769 Wesley sent his first official representatives to America, Richard Boardman and Joseph Pilmoor. By 1771, with Methodism gaining converts, Wesley asked for more volunteers to go to America. Five men were selected, including the 26-year-old Francis Asbury.

Asbury, a native of Handsworth, near Birmingham, England,

*Francis Asbury*

had been raised in a devout Christian home, but had not been converted until about the age of 15, when he attended a Methodist meeting. Not long thereafter he began preaching, and was accepted by Wesley as a lay preacher in 1767.

Within two years of arriving in Philadelphia, Asbury became head of the Methodist Baltimore District. He would devote the rest of his life to preaching, riding nearly 300,000 miles on horseback, from Maine to Georgia and as far west as Kentucky, delivering more than 16,000 sermons.

The movement spread southward. According to W. L. Grissom's *History of Methodism in North Carolina* (Vol. I), Joseph Pilmoor was the first missionary sent by John Wesley to enter North Carolina, coming in 1772. But Asbury was not long behind, visiting North Carolina 72 times from 1780 until the year of his death, 1816. He preached several times in the Waxhaw area.

Methodism first gained a following among English settlers in eastern North Carolina, where it coexisted with the Anglican church. It was not uncommon for Methodists and Anglicans to share church buildings, and even clergymen.

Even before the Methodist movement in America became a church, its work was planned and coordinated at an annual conference of preachers.

The first conference was held July 14, 1773, in Philadelphia. At the time, Methodism had a total of ten traveling preachers, and of those, only six or seven attended the conference. There were six circuits: New York, New Jersey, Philadelphia, Baltimore, Norfolk and Petersburg. The number of members "in society" was 1160, nearly half of whom were in Maryland. In all of Virginia, there were 100 enrolled Methodists.[4] Subsequent conferences were held yearly thereafter.

At the time of the American Revolution, there was still no organized Methodist denomination in America, although a number of Methodist societies had been formed. Because of their ties to England, Methodist preachers were not popular during the war. Francis Asbury was the only British Methodist preacher to remain in America.

Even had there been no Revolution, American Methodism seemed destined to become a distinct church at some point, perhaps after the death of Wesley. But with the Revolution it became a virtual necessity. Almost none of Wesley's Methodist preachers were ordained, and thus could not perform the sacraments of baptism and communion. Wesley had always regarded his followers as being members of the Church of England, and he expected them to attend the Anglican Church for the sacraments.

After the Revolution, the Anglican Church, officially headed by the English king, no longer had official standing in America. Even before the war, ordained Anglican clergy were few in number, leaving most Methodists without a means to receive baptism or communion. Methodist preachers in America were already clamoring for ordination. Some had even ordained each other and began administering the sacraments. They were persuaded to suspend their plan for a year until John Wesley could be consulted.

In September 1784 John Wesley gave his approval for a new church to be formed. In a letter addressed "To Dr. Coke, Mr. Asbury, and our brethren in North America," he appointed Thomas Coke and Francis Asbury as joint superintendents, and concluded: "As our American brethren are now totally disentangled both from the state, and from the English hierarchy, we dare not entangle them again, either with the one or the other. They are now at full liberty, simply to follow the scriptures and the primitive church. And we judge it best that they should stand fast in that liberty, wherewith God has so strangely made them free."[5]

Methodists in America date their formal existence from a meeting called the "Christmas Conference" in Baltimore on December 24, 1784, when about 60 ministers established the Methodist Episcopal Church. The word "episcopal" refers to a church governed by bishops, although Wesley preferred the term "superintendent." Coke had already been consecrated as superintendent by Wesley. At Wesley's direction, he now ordained Asbury to share the office. Asbury would later change the title to "bishop."

At the time the Methodist Episcopal Church was established, the movement had grown to 46 circuits with 83 traveling preachers.[7] Already, it was taking root in North Carolina.

## Chapter Notes

1.  Elmer T. Clark, *Methodism in Western North Carolina,* p. 14.
2.  Accounts of the establishment of of the first Wesleyan sociaties in New York, Baltimore and Philadelphia may be found in numerous publications, including the *Discipline,* and footnotes by Elmer T. Clark in the Epworth/Abingdon edition of Asbury's *Journal.*
3.  In Chapter 12 of his Methodist history Lee lists all preachers admitted to the traveling connection from 1773 to 1806, and a list of those who were only probationers. Strawbridge is on the latter list.
4.  Lee, p. 49.
5.  *Ibid.,* pp. 91-92. Lee provides a partial text of the letter. The full letter may be found in Vol. 3 of *The Journals and Letters of Francis Asbury,* edited by Elmer T. Clark, p. 37. It is interesting to note that Lee's version of the letter, presumably taken from the minutes of the 1784 conference, omits a part of the fourth paragraph in which Wesley recommends use of a liturgy similar to that of the Church of England. The leaders of the American movement were not enthusiastic about using the English liturgy, and must have edited the letter for that reason.
6.  *Ibid.,* p. 87.

# 3

# Charlotte Town

In the 1700s Great Britain had begun promoting settlement in its hitherto neglected southern colonies in America. In North Carolina the promise of cheap land and a favorable climate began to attract a steady stream of settlers, primarily Scots-Irish and Germans, from Delaware, Maryland and Pennsylvania, migrating southward down the Great Wagon Road that led from Pennsylvania through Virginia's Shenandoah valley and into the region now known as the Piedmont Crescent of North Carolina. Others, including Swiss and French Huguenots, came up from South Carolina, following the great Pee Dee and Catawba rivers northwestward from Charleston.[1]

It is said that the first white settler in what is now Charlotte was Thomas Spratt, who journeyed down the Great Wagon Road with his wife and 19-year-old daughter, Susannah, about 1753. Spratt built his cabin off present-day Providence Road, near Crescent Avenue, just beyond the future site of Presbyterian Hospital. But it was Susannah's suitor, the 21-year-old Thomas Polk, who claimed the distinction of being the first true Charlottean.

Polk chose to build a home for himself and his new bride a discreet two miles away, on a slight rise at the crossing of two Indian trading paths. It was largely through Polk's influence and labor that the trails would someday become Tryon and Trade Streets, the heart of the Carolinas' metropolis, Charlotte.

History books tell us that Polk's home was the finest in the whole village, indeed the only painted house on the street. This home would later be used as a headquarters by British General Cornwallis during his two-week occupation of Charlotte in 1780. After the war, in 1791, it was the scene of a festive dinner for President George Washington on his southern tour.

But this probably was not Polk's first home. Most likely Polk, a young man newly arrived in this lonely outpost, would have assembled his first home from logs harvested on the surrounding slopes. The fine house would almost surely have been a later accomplishment, perhaps using clapboards sawed in a water-powered mill a few miles away. The home survived in Charlotte for many years, and later housed a cigar factory.

In 1762 the Provincial Assembly carved off a portion of western Anson County to create Mecklenburg County. In a campaign to have

*Charlotte in 1775*

*The photo above depicts Charlotte as it may have appeared in the year of the Mecklenburg Declaration of Independence. This would be the view from a point approximately above the present day Discovery Place parking deck at Church and Sixth Streets. The numbered points of interest are: 1. Thomas Polk's residence; 2. county courthouse, where the Mecklenburg Declaration of Independence was adopted; 3. Queens Museum, also known as Liberty Hall, a school for boys; 4. Pat Jack's Tavern, a popular gathering place of the time; and 5. blacksmith shop, future site of the town church, and later, First Presbyterian Church. A sketch in the September 1, 1970 Charlotte Observer shows Duncan Ochiltree's store on the corner diagonally across from Polk's home. This image is based on a diorama at the Charlotte Museum of History.*

his crossroads village designated the county seat, Polk and some friends built a courthouse in the square adjoining his home.

In 1767 Henry McCulloh, agent for Lord George Augustus Selwyn, deeded 360 acres for a town, naming Polk, Abraham Alexander and John Frohock of Rowan County as trustees. The plot described in the deed was a slightly skewed square, exactly "240 poles" (3960 feet, or three quarters of a mile) on each side, centered on Polk's residence and the courthouse.[2] The plot, with its curious tilt of 40 degrees from true north, reflected the orientation of the original trading path intersection on which Charlotte was built. Today the street

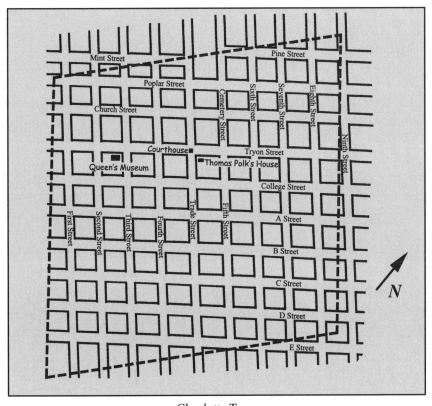

*Charlotte Town*
*This map shows the approximate city limits of Charlotte as conveyed in the 1767 deed from Lord George Augustus Selwyn. Streets which did not exist at that time are shown here for reference purposes only.*

grid of uptown Charlotte still confuses visitors who wonder why North Tryon Street does not really go north.

Charlotte was named for Queen Charlotte, the German bride of King George III, and Mecklenburg County was named for Queen Charlotte's homeland in Germany. The naming sequence is puzzling, however, because Mecklenburg County was formed in 1762 and Charlotte was not incorporated until 1768. However, there are references to "Charlottetown" prior to 1768, giving rise to the supposition that Polk and his friends had already bestowed the Queen's name on their village well before its incorporation, perhaps even before the county was formed.[3] In such case it would have been natural to seek further appeasement of the monarch in choosing a name for the county. Although the naming selections did not achieve their supposed purpose—gaining the King's favor—they did spare us an alternative possibility. The town could have been called "Polk's Crossroads!"

Charlotte remained about this size for well over 100 years. In the mid-1800s the town was divided into four election districts, called "wards," with Tryon and Trade Streets serving as boundaries. While the wards no longer have legal status, the names survive and are commonly used to identify the four distinct quadrants of the center city.

In 1885 the corporate limits were extended by a few blocks in each direction, to take in virtually all of the area regarded today as "uptown."

Most, if not all of Mecklenburg's first settlers were Presbyterians, following the historic faith of their Scottish ancestors. Their first order of business, after staking out their homesteads, was setting up churches. Rocky River, in what is now Cabarrus County, was established in 1748 (some accounts say 1751). Sugaw Creek became a sister church of Rocky River in 1755, followed by Steel Creek in 1760, Hopewell, 1762; Poplar Tent (now in Cabarrus County, 1764; Providence, 1767; and Philadelphia, originally known as Clear Creek, 1770.[4] Other nearby churches included the Old Waxhaw Church near Lancaster, 1755; and Centre, in Iredell County, 1765.

The area's first Lutheran churches were built in what is now Cabarrus County. Although Mecklenburg had been designated as St. Martin's Parish of the Anglican Church, there is no record of a congregation being formed in the county.[5]

The Methodist movement, just getting started in England, was not yet officially a separate denomination, and would not gain a foothold in Mecklenburg until about 1785.

Early Methodists and Presbyterians had a curious relationship. We find instances where the two groups showed warm cooperation; and others where they were bitter rivals.

Methodists were castigated from the Presbyterian pulpit. The faithful were exhorted to stay away from the Wesleyan revivals, and roundly censured when they went anyway. Some were even cast out of their churches for attending Methodist meetings.

An example of Presbyterian sentiment of that day may be found in a resolution adopted by Session XXI of the Presbyterian Synod, meeting at Sugaw Creek Church Oct. 6, 1808:

> Whereas, the Methodist Church embraces doctrines that we are far from considering orthodox, and as they are in the habit of insinuating that Presbyterian ministers are mercenary in their calling, of speaking disrespectfully of our church, and endeavoring to withdraw members from our communion; therefore, to avoid all feuds, animosities and contentions with that people, the Synod recommend that all unnecessary intercourse with them be avoided, that our brethren in the ministry be careful to teach all the doctrines of our holy religion as contained in our Confession of Faith and Catechism; and at particular times, when prudence and duty may direct, to explain and establish those doctrines, which we believe the church alluded to has misunderstood, if not perverted."

The resolution included a provision that Presbyterians who invited Methodists to preach in their churches without approval of the session be "dealt with by their respective sessions as disorderly."[6]

Against this backdrop, it is especially interesting to note that, 200 years later, Methodists and Presbyterians are the closest of friends, cooperate on countless endeavors, and the average person would be hard put to identify any point of contention between them.

## Chapter Notes

1. LeGette Blythe and Charles Brockmann, *Hornets' Nest,* p. 17.
2. In specifying the 40 degree tilt, the deed-writers were a bit off, since the boundary lines do not exactly parallel any of the streets. The original corners were marked by trees—a white oak, a pine, a hickory and a black oak—all of which are long gone. We can reasonably guess the location of boundaries, however, by reference to the layout of streets. If we assume the Square was centered on the Tryon Street axis, then First Street would be just inside the southern boundary, which is logical, and Eighth Street would be just inside the northern boundary. On the other hand, it appears from the way streets were laid out that the original town limits extended farther to the east than to the west from the Square. The systematic naming of streets going east from the Square extends (after College Street) from "A" Street through "E" Street. On the west side, streets are named for trees (Poplar and Pine), but this system extends only two blocks beyond Church Street. This centering of the town east of the Square was evidently related to land Thomas Polk had previously staked out in what is now First Ward, extending to a line near the intersection of Eighth and Davidson Streets. Some writers say that the boundaries were not strictly observed; that the town may have actually received a bit more land than described in the deed. The deed is recorded in Deed Book 9, page 317, in the Mecklenburg County Register of Deeds Office.
3. Blythe and Brockmann, p. 162.
4. Mary Norton Kratt, *Charlotte, Spirit of the New South,* p. 24.
5. The parish designation was made at the time the county was created. Generally, each county was considered a separate parish of the state church.
6. William Henry Foote, Sketches of North Carolina, p. 462.

# 4

# Camp Meetings

In the early days camp meetings were a popular form of religious revival. Some people believe they started in Kentucky, Tennessee or South Carolina. But in his *History of Methodism in North Carolina*, W. L. Grissom contends the camp meeting had its beginning in North Carolina.

The great revivalist John McGee held a camp meeting in Lincoln County about 1790. Daniel Asbury, involved in that meeting, set up a second one in 1794, at Rehobeth, in what is now Catwaba County. William McKendree was one of the preachers. The Rock Springs Camp Ground at Denver is an outgrowth of that Rehobeth camp meeting.[1]

Jesse Lee, in his history of Methodism, suggests the "camping" aspect of the meetings developed out of necessity. Paraphrasing from Lee, so many people attended the meetings, no building was big enough to hold them. The preachers were forced to conduct their services outdoors. The meetings could last three or four days, and if the spirit became intense, preaching might last through the night. Moreover, as Lee puts it, "In some cases persons were struck down by the power of God, and lay helpless most part of the night and could not be taken away." Of course, their friends had to stay with them until the rapture subsided.

Thus, people began to come prepared with several day's supply of food for themselves and their horses, as well as provisions for making a shelter under the stars.

Lee concludes, "As the people were invited to come to encamp on the ground, they soon gave those meetings the distinguishing name of camp meetings."[2]

Referring to the importance of camp meetings, Grissom says "[Methodism's] early history is the history of a great revival movement."

Often the meetings would be a joint effort of Methodists, Baptists and Presbyterians, with a dozen or more preachers taking part. In the earliest days Presbyterians would often organize the camp meetings, but they soon became a centerpiece of the Methodist movement. Methodist author Albert Deems Betts comments, "...the Presbyterians began to shy away from [camp meetings] because of the seeming lack of order, for the Methodist preachers and people were very demonstrative."[3]

A camp meeting would last several days, with prayers, singing and thunderous sermons continuing late into the night, resuming the following morning. For what little sleep people might get, rough shelters, now commonly known as "tents," would be erected around the central gathering area. Sometimes the central speaking place would be a brush arbor, but with crowds numbering in the thousands, no arbor could hold them all. Some accounts describe simultaneous meetings being conducted by different preachers at different "stands" around the camp.

A camp meeting near the end of March 1802 has been described in a number of books and articles. A Presbyterian minister, Rev. James Hall, quoted in Foote's *Sketches of North Carolina*, says the meeting was held in lower Mecklenburg County, near the state line, with an estimated 6,000 persons attending. "Twelve Presbyterian ministers, one Baptist and one Methodist attended. Worship began, as usual, on Friday, and continued until near noon on Tuesday. Never did I see a set of men labor with more assiduity than the ministers labored from Friday noon until Sabbath night at 9 o'clock..."

In her book, *The Waxhaws*, Louise Pettus writes, "Reverend Richard Furman, an eminent Baptist who was present, counted 120 wagons, twenty carts, and eight carriages. Tents encircled an open space about 150 yards by 300 yards near a stream. An estimated three to five thousand people attended."

James Jenkins, in a letter to Francis Asbury in June 1802, described a "general meeting, led by the Presbyterians," with five Methodist, five Baptist, and twelve Presbyterian ministers. "The Lord was present, and wrought for his own glory. Sinners were converted on all sides, and numbers found the Lord."

Despite the disparity of numbers, all these accounts may be about the same camp meeting. Until 1842 that section of Union County including the present town of Waxhaw was still a part of Mecklenburg County, and thus could have been referred to as "lower Mecklenburg." The Old Waxhaw Presbyterian Church of which Louise Pettus writes is in Lancaster County, South Carolina, but still within that entire section still known as "the Waxhaws."

It became commonplace in camp meetings for some worshippers to became "exercised." Foote describes the experience: "...persons began to be struck down during religious exercises, lying like persons in a swoon for a length of time; then rise with songs of praise for the deliverance they had experienced of a spiritual nature." Sometimes there would be great thrashing about. Another writer says that the vegetation beneath a person being "exercised" would be torn up for several feet around.

Another camp meeting, also about 1802 in Anson County, is described in an article by Samuel Leard in *The Southern Christian Advocate* for July and August, 1846. It was copied from microfilm records at the World Methodist Building, Lake Junaluska, by The Rev. John A. Petty. Leard says six Methodist and three Baptist ministers led the services. The following are excepts from Leard's account:

> The people came on their own hook and brought their wallets, bags, and pockets well stored with provisions. They came with their wagons and carts and on horseback and a great many came on foot from a distance with their provisions on their shoulders. There were

three tents, one of poles and two of rails. The other places of shelter were booths made of bushes.

There were two stands about 150 yards apart and it appears that the two denominations labored together and were friendly. They preached, exhorted, and prayed as with the Holy Ghost sent down from above, and the power of the Lord took hold on the people.

The ground was literally covered with the 'slain of the Lord.' There was a signal display of the power of God under the preaching of the venerable Father Ledbetter. He was then in his prime and his voice filled the forest. As to the number of conversions we know not, but there were many.

Leard describes the "dancing" that took place:

It was commonly regarded in that day as the results of the Holy Spirit operating on the body as well as the soul or rather influencing the body through the medium of the soul. Again it usually attended revivals and seemed to increase in frequency and power as a revival of religion was found to spread and become deeper and more solemn in its character. Again, persons of unquestioned piety were affected in this way so that it could not be said always or even generally assumed to be for hypocritical purposes. It is even probable that in that day such an exercise was regarded as evidence of superior devotion to God. With how much truth we will not pretend to say. From the best accounts we have it certainly was involuntary, rather an object of fear than desire.

Another manifestation was commonly called "the jerks," and Leard identified three distinct variations:

The jerks may be divided into at least three varieties. The first was what we shall denominate the 'long jerk.' In this the head was brought with violence toward the ground in front and then by a sudden reaction it would be thrown back within a short distance of the earth in the rear. This was by far the most violent kind and would convey to the mind of the spectator the idea of an automaton filled with springs of unusual elasticity. Sometimes it would seize with violence on the feet and limbs and then Saint Vitus' Dance might stand back and look on with admiration. With colored people under such circumstances, the earth received a sound thrashing and vegetation sighed and expired for several feet around.

The second variety we shall call the quick or short jerk. This was an involuntary and sudden motion of the head forward or to one side without much affecting the body, accompanied with a sudden snapping of the eyelids and contortion of the features.

The third variety was well known among the people as the barking jerks...

Leard says he never had the opportunity to witness the "barking jerks," so we may never know what the "barking jerk" was, but we can imagine.[4]

Originally staged as one-time revivals, the camp meetings became recurring annual events, and were major religious and social functions. The makeshift outdoor setting may have added to their appeal. It is interesting that the camp grounds were traditionally chosen by the presiding elders, traveling preachers and lay leaders for the fall gathering of their quarterly conferences. Through much of the 1820s and 1830s meetings of the circuit covering Mecklenburg were held each September at Moore's and later the Big Spring Camp Ground.[5] Moore's was established by Andrew Moore, a leading figure in Mecklenburg's Methodist movement in those early days, as well as a founder of the Bethesda society which was a forerunner of today's Asbury United Methodist Church.

Big Spring Camp was on Dowd Road, at one time a main road from Charlotte to Dallas in Gaston County. Land for the campground was purchased in 1834 by Thomas McDonald, William Williams and Brawley Oates, trustees for the campground. The tract was described in the deed as 26 acres, more or less. About 1836 a "harbor" (arbor) had been built there. In 1912 Big Spring Church celebrated the one hundredth anniversary of the camp meeting.[6]

Even today the camps remain popular. Two well-known camp meetings still held in the Charlotte area are Balls Creek, in Catawba County, and Rock Springs, as mentioned earlier, in Lincoln County near Denver.

## Chapter Notes

1.  Elmer Clark, *Methodism in Western North Carolina*, pp. 30-31. Though Rehobeth is now in Catawba County, it would have been part of Lincoln in 1790. Lincoln County was formed in 1779, encompassing what is now Lincoln and Catawba. Catawba County was separated in 1842.
2.  Jesse Lee, *A Short History of the Methodists in the United States of America*, p. 279.
3.  Albert Deems Betts, *History of South Carolina Methodism*, p. 161.
4.  A similar description of "the jerks" is found in Moore, *Pioneers of Methodism in North Carolina and Virginia,* pp. 176-177.
5.  Minutes of Quarterly Conferences of the Sugar Creek and Charlotte Circuits.
6.  Unpublished history of Big Spring UMC.

# 5

# Mecklenburg's First Methodists

Looking at today's soaring skyline and humming freeways, it is hard to believe that Charlotte was not always the commercial and cultural hub of the southern Piedmont. Yet, as President Washington so aptly put it in 1791, Charlotte in its earliest days was a "trifling place," so trifling, in fact, that only scant notice is taken of it in the journals of the first Methodist visitors to North Carolina. Charlotte was rarely a destination; seldom even a stopping point. Francis Asbury, who crisscrossed North Carolina repeatedly, barely mentions that he "passed Charlotte" in March 1794, on his way from the Waxhaw area to a meeting with Daniel Asbury, in Lincoln County.

His journal entries, in the quaint style of his day, provide a graphic image of conditions faced by those pioneer preachers:

> Saturday, 15. We set out under discouraging prospects; having had a heavy rain the night before. We came to Shepherds, where we had to swim our horses alongside a canoe, and had they not struggled powerfully and freed themselves, from among the bushes and grapevines, they had certainly drowned [sic]; we returned across the stream, and then brought them down the creek, to a place where there were no trees in the way, and we got safe across.
>
> Sunday, 16. The waters being still high, our passage difficult, and having no inclination to travel on the Sabbath, we continued at Shepherd's, where we stayed the night before. Notice we circulated through the neighborhood, and by eleven o'clock there was collected a congregation of sixty or seventy people.
>
> Monday, 17. We set out, and passed Charlotte, in Mecklenburg...[1]

The Shepherd home, where Asbury stayed, is thought to have been near the present Mecklenburg-Union County line. The present-day route from Waxhaw into Charlotte is N.C. Highway 16, which crosses Sixmile Creek at the county line. This is very likely near the spot where Asbury had trouble crossing the flooded stream. Since Union was still a part of Mecklenburg County at that time, Asbury's sermon at Shepherd's in March 1794 could be the first Methodist sermon in Mecklenburg for which we have a written record.

On another of Asbury's trips through the region, in January 1808, he spent a night with John McKamie Wilson, pastor of Philadelphia Presbyterian Church in Mint Hill. Asbury writes that he was "comfortably and kindly accommodated," but he did not record preaching during the visit.[2]

Perhaps one reason Charlotte was not a prime target for early evangelism was the well-known fact that Presbyterians already had a lock on the place. When Methodists traveled in North Carolina, it was mostly in the eastern part of the state.

Methodism was firmly planted in Virginia before spreading into the Carolinas. Norfolk, Virginia's major port city, was a center of Methodist activity. Brunswick County, on the state line in south central Virginia, was one of the commonwealth's most prominent Methodist circuits. Initially, the Brunswick Circuit encompassed parts of North Carolina.

Joseph Pilmoor is considered the first Methodist to preach in North Carolina (in 1772)[3], but there is no record that he formed a society here. Robert Williams is credited with organizing the first Methodist society to be located in North Carolina.[4] The Carolina Circuit, the state's first, was formed in 1776. It was served by Edward Dromgoole, Francis Poythress, and Isham Tatum.[5] According to conference records, there were already 683 Methodists in North Carolina by the time Poythress, Dromgoole and Tatum began their labors here. In 1778 the Carolina Circuit (later called "North Carolina") was supplanted by three circuits within the state, Roanoke, Tar River and New Hope. The Yadkin Circuit appeared in 1780.[6] At the time it was formed, the Yadkin Circuit extended (theoretically) all the way to the Blue Ridge Mountains. In 1785, Henry Willis was the elder in charge; Henry Bingham and Thomas Williamson were the preachers.[7]

Boundaries for the circuits were not clearly established, but the Yadkin Circuit theoretically included Mecklenburg County. However, there is no record of preachers from that circuit working in the Charlotte area.

It is commonly accepted that Mecklenburg's first organized Methodist society was the gathering of about 1785 which became known as Harrison's and survives today as Harrison United Methodist Church, near the state line south of Pineville. Harrison's was identified as a "preaching place" on the Santee Circuit of South Carolina.[8]

The Rev. G. W. Bumgarner, a noted authority on Methodist history in Mecklenburg County, reports what may have been the earliest Methodist sermon in the town of Charlotte. It was delivered at the courthouse on the Square in 1805 by the evangelist Lorenzo Dow, and probably was not a high point for local Methodism. As Dow himself would later write, some people "strove to kick up a dust."[9] Dow, a native of Rhode Island, had left his circuit and evidently was a freelance preacher at the time of his Charlotte appearance. He was widely known as an eccentric, which could explain his lukewarm reception in Charlotte.

Methodist preaching became a recurring event in Charlotte after 1814, with the arrival of a physician, Dr. David Dunlap. As described elsewhere, Dr. Dunlap, a devout Methodist converted from the Presbyterian faith, made a habit of inviting itinerant preachers to deliver sermons in Charlotte. Among them, two whose names have been recorded were William Terry and Jonathan Jackson.

William Terry was a local preacher from Fayetteville.[10] Little else is known of him. Jonathan Jackson was well known in Methodist circles, having joined the traveling connection in 1789. He had served on circuits in both Carolinas, Georgia and Virginia, and was serving on the Lincoln Circuit in 1814.[11]

By the latter part of 1814 the Methodists had established the Sugar Creek Circuit, which covered much of Mecklenburg County. William Barnett was the preacher in charge, and Charlotte became a regular stop on the circuit.[12] Samuel Harrison, whose family may have provided the name for Harrison Church, was a local preacher. Harrison had been admitted to the traveling ministry in 1808 and was first appointed to the Rocky River Circuit. He was the first preacher who called on Margaret Kerr Martin and helped organize a society which eventually became Trinity UMC, on Beatties Ford Road.

It was during this period that several new congregations were organized, including one known first as Christenburys, and later, Bethesda, which, in turn, was a parent of today's Asbury United Methodist Church.

The Sugar Creek Circuit was part of the Catawba District, of which Daniel Asbury was presiding elder. While they shared a last name, there is no evidence that Daniel and Francis Asbury were related, although they were well acquainted.[13] Daniel Asbury was one of the best known Methodist leaders to have an early association with Mecklenburg County.

His story is a remarkable one, worthy of a book in itself. Daniel was born February 18, 1762, in Fairfax County, Virginia. When he was about 16 years old he was captured by a band of Shawnee Indians and taken to the far West. He learned the Shawnee language, was adopted (one version says by an old chief) and was well treated, but nonetheless suffered greatly in the primitive lifestyle. The War of Independence was underway, and at some point he was taken prisoner by a British force, who held him in chains in Detroit. Eventually Daniel made his escape (or was freed, according to some accounts), and began the long journey home to Virginia. At first his mother didn't recognize him, now a young man of 21. When she did, her joy can only be imagined.[14]

As a boy, Asbury's religious training had been sadly lacking, and years of hardship did nothing to soften his soul. But now, back home, he was led to a spiritual awakening by Methodist preachers, and he became a Methodist. He was received into the traveling connection in 1786. His first appointment was in Virginia, but after three years he was working in the Yadkin, Catawba and Lincoln circuits. It was Asbury, in fact, who organized the Lincoln Circuit in Lincoln and Catawba counties. Reportedly, he found there a settlement of people who were already Methodists, who had moved from the Brunswick area in Virginia.[15] In 1790 he married Nancy Morris and had a son, named Henry,[16] who later became a Methodist minister. It was about this time that he founded the Rehobeth society. A marker there identifies it as the oldest Methodist church in North Carolina west of the Catawba.

Daniel "located" in Lincoln until 1800, when he was readmitted to the connection and appointed to the Union Circuit. Following this, he served a number of circuits, including Yadkin, 1801-02; Union, 1803; was named presiding elder of the Catawba District in 1814-1817; was back in Lincoln, 1822-23; and returned to the Sugar Creek Circuit as traveling preacher in 1824. After a long and fruitful career he died on Sunday, April 15, 1825. He is buried at Rehobeth Church in Catawba County.[17]

Another name well known to students of Methodist history is that of the Rev. James Jenkins. He began preaching in 1792 and was ordained a deacon by Francis Asbury during a conference at the Finch residence in Newberry County, South Carolina in December 1793.[18]

According to Moore, Jenkins was one of a class of preachers known as "Sons of Thunder" for their energetic oratory and commanding personalities. Other nicknames for Jenkins included "Thundering Jimmy" and "Bawling Jimmy."[19] In 1801 Jenkins was presiding elder of the South Carolina District. His final service was in the Wateree Circuit 1812-13, when he retired. He remained on the rolls of the South Carolina Conference in a superannuated relationship until 1847.[20] Jenkins kept a journal of his travels, which, together with his letters, is a source of much valuable information about Methodist work during that period.

# Chapter Notes

1. Francis Asbury, *Journal,* Vol. II, p. 8.
2. *Ibid.*, p. 564. Note that other histories spell Wilson's middle name "Makemie." In his book, *The Presbyterian Gathering on Clear Creek*, Russell Martin Kerr relates that Wilson had been influenced by a Wesley-inspired revival while a student at Hampden-Sydney College (pp. 110-111). This may account for Wilson's friendliness toward Asbury.
3. Elmer T. Clark, *Methodism in Western North Carolina,* p. 15.
4. M. H. Moore, *Pioneers of Methodism in North Carolina and Virginia,* p. 47.
5. Clark, p. 15.
6. Jesse Lee, A Short History of the Methodists in the United States of America, p. 63.
7. Clark, p. 26.
8. This information is based on various histories of Harrison Church. The South Carolina Conference does not have records of the Santee Circuit prior to 1813.
9. W. L. Grissom, *History of Methodism in North Carolina,* p. 324. The quote appears to have come from Dow's memoirs. Several writers refer to Dow as "the eccentric Lorenzo Dow," and one calls him "crazy Lorenzo Dow."
10. Mildred Morse McEwen, *First United Methodist Church,* p. 14.
11. Asbury, p. 178 (footnote) and p. 763 (footnote).
12. Journal of the Sugar Creek Circuit. Charlotte appears regularly in the minutes through May 30, 1817, and then is not mentioned again until 1820. This "gap" includes the period when, according to Jenkins, David Dunlap organized the society in Charlotte, of which he was the class leader. Several times during the "gap," Dunlap attended the quarterly circuit meetings as a class leader, even though Charlotte is not mentioned as a preaching place, but he could have been representing the Buckhill society. It is possible that Charlotte was simply not mentioned in the minutes, although it would be odd to be overlooked continuously for three years.
13. Asbury, *Journal,* Vol. I, pp. 3-4.
14. Moore, pp.169-172.
15. Moore, p. 172.
16. Asbury, *Journal,* Vol. III, p. 543 (footnote).
17. Clark, p. 171.
18. Asbury, Vol. I, p. 798.
19. Moore, p. 255
20. *Ibid.*

# 6

# Harrison's Church

In 1785 the American Revolution was fresh in the memory of Mecklenburg County residents. England had signed the final peace treaty and withdrawn its troops from New York just two years earlier. It would be another two years before the U.S. Constitution was written.

Life was returning to normal in Charlotte, still a village crossroads covering less than a square mile with a few homes and stores, a flour mill, and a blacksmith shop.

Mecklenburg was still almost exclusively Presbyterian, the faithful attending one of the seven churches surrounding the little village of Charlotte. Followers of John Wesley had begun to attract converts in the Carolinas, although the Methodist Episcopal Church, as a denomination, had been formally established only a year earlier, in 1784. The Carolina Circuit, embracing most of North and South Carolina, had been organized in 1776. There is no record, however, of regular Methodist preaching in Mecklenburg County at that time.

By all accounts, the earliest Methodist activity in Mecklenburg County was in an area south of Pineville, near the South Carolina state line, about 1785. Tradition holds that the congregation was organized by James David Jonathan and Daniel Mills. Jonathan, known as "Uncle Johnny," was the licensed exhorter. "Uncle Daniel" was class leader. The two men would lead worship services when the circuit-riding preacher was not available. No records have come to light to document this account, but it has been accepted for over 100 years, and we have no reason to question it.[1]

Orion Hutchinson, who has compiled an excellent history of
Harrison Church, finds additional evidence of Harrison's early origin
in the work of noted Methodist historian Albert Shipp. Shipp reports
that, when formed in 1786, the Santee Circuit of South Carolina "came
to Providence, within 10 miles of Charlotte."[2] Hutchinson concludes,
for the circuit to extend this far northward, there must have been a
preaching place in the vicinity.

The story of how this first fellowship of Methodists came to be
formed in a staunchly Presbyterian county has been lost in the passage
of time. It could be that people who were already Methodists settled
there and provided the original spark. According to Jesse Lee, some
Methodists left their established homes during the American
Revolution to seek a safer environment. This would have been in the
period of 1775 to 1783. Conceivably, some could have moved to
southern Mecklenburg and organized a society among themselves.

Or, it may have been simply a matter of economics. As Alexander
relates, people in that part of the county who had means of
transportation would travel to Providence Church, some seven miles
distant. Those who had neither a carriage nor suitable horse for the
journey would stay closer home to engage in worship. Even then
Methodism reached out to the poor and unchurched, reinforcing the
popular view that it was a religion for the lower classes. As Alexander
put it, "the best of society were ashamed to be seen at Harrison."[3]

For at least 20 years the congregation met in a brush arbor, but
sometime between 1805 and 1815 decided to erect their first
permanent building. A wealthy Presbyterian, Harrison Hood, had
befriended the little Methodist fellowship and supported their decision.
He agreed to donate land and materials to build a small church. He
even assigned workers from his own farm to help build it. The little
rectangular meeting house, about 40 feet long and 30 feet wide, was
constructed of logs with a large batten door at one end. Hood is said
to have attended services at the new church and may have been a
member for a time.[4]

From its beginning Harrison had been associated with circuits
in upper South Carolina. In 1815 it became a part of the newly-

formed Sugar Creek Circuit, for the first time joining other Mecklenburg County congregations including Martin's (later to become Buckhill, then Trinity) and Charlotte. In 1834 the name of the Sugar Creek Circuit was changed to Charlotte Circuit.

In 1840 the original log church was destroyed by fire and eight years later a new frame building was erected. In 1902 The church began work on its third sanctuary, which was completed and dedicated the following year. This building, a frame structure in the Victorian in style, was described as "the finest example of its architectural genre" among Methodist churches in Mecklenburg County. Tragically, the building was destroyed by fire on March 17, 1984.

It would be interesting to know more about the founders of Harrison Church, and circumstances surrounding its beginnings.

*This Harrison Church building, erected in 1902, served the congregation until it was destroyed by fire in 1984.*

However, the search for more details has been disappointing. The names of James Jonathan and Daniel Mills, organizers of the first society, have not turned up in a search of non-church records from that period. They do not appear in the 1790 census of Mecklenburg County. The South Carolina United Methodist Conference does not have minutes of the Santee or Wateree Circuits prior to 1813.

Perhaps the scarcity of information may stem in part from the church's location. The area surrounding today's Harrison Church has a long and curious history.

Originally the Catawba Indian nation occupied most of the territory along the banks of the nearby river which bears their name. As European settlers began to arrive, the Catawbas withdrew to an ever-shrinking area south of the present state line in the what is now York and Lancaster Counties, South Carolina. In July 1763 a diamond-shaped tract of 144,000 acres, 15 miles on each side, was set aside for the Catawbas by King George III as part of the Treaty of Pine Tree Hill.[5] The area came to be known as "Indian Land." The trail leading southward from Charlotte through the Indian Land took travelers to Lancaster and would some day be known as U.S. 521. A corner of the old reservation boundary remains today as a part of the line between Mecklenburg, York, and Lancaster counties.

The Catawbas were a peaceful and friendly people, and entirely too cooperative for their own good. As time passed, they surrendered or bartered away much of their land to the white newcomers. In what is known as the Nation Ford Treaty of 1840 the tribe sold its land to the state of South Carolina, enabling white settlers to acquire legal ownership of it.[6]

At one time the entire area was in dispute between the two states. When North and South Carolina were divided in 1712, it was understood that the dividing line would be the 35th parallel, which passes through present-day Monroe and touches the southernmost corner of Mecklenburg County. The border was intended to extend westward along this parallel "to the South Seas" (the Pacific Ocean). However, as of the mid-1700s, the line had not been surveyed or marked off. Landowners in the area between Charlotte and Lancaster never knew for sure which state they were in, and might declare themselves residents of either state, depending on which domicile was, for the moment, more advantageous. Thus it is plausible that people living in that area might not appear in Mecklenburg records.

The story of how Harrison Church got its name illustrates the problem of documenting church history. Did the church get its name from Harrison Hood, donor of land and materials for the first building? Or was it named for a family whose last name was Harrison, or for a well-known preacher who settled near there before the church built its first building?

Many of the earliest Methodist societies began meeting in members' homes, and often took the name of the host family. There is evidence that a man named Isaiah Harrison and his family had settled in the area sometime prior to 1790. President George Washington, passing through in 1791 on his way from Camden to Charlotte, mentions in his diary that he stopped for breakfast at "Harrison's."[7]

The Rev. Samuel Harrison, a preacher of note in early Mecklenburg, settled in that section of lower Mecklenburg about 1811, perhaps because relatives already lived there. Some sources suggest that Samuel Harrison's father was named Isaiah, but nothing has been found to document a link between the Reverend Harrison and the Harrison visited by Washington.

The Harrisons are linked with another prominent Mecklenburg family, the Hoods of Mint Hill. Tunis (Theunis) Hood, patriarch of the Hood clan, was married to an Elizabeth Harrison before moving to Mecklenburg. Their son, Tunis, Jr., also married a Harrison, and this no doubt is the source of the middle name of Tunis' grandson, John Harrison Hood.

Harrison, as he was called, married Socelia Black, daughter of Sophia Springs Black. Members of the Springs family were among those who had come into possession of "Indian land" through government grants. Thus it was through Socelia's uncle, Major Richard Springs, that Harrison Hood acquired a large tract of land which included the arbor where the forebears of Harrison Church had been worshipping.[8] When the small congregation desired to build a permanent structure, Harrison Hood, as mentioned previously, donated land, timber and the labor of slaves from his farm to build it.

Some have speculated that the "Harrison's" mentioned by Washington could have been the home of Harrison Hood, but it is unlikely the President would have referred to the host by his first name. It is far more likely that Washington's mention of "Harrison's" would refer to the abode of someone whose last name was Harrison.

Even so, whether the church was named for a Harrison family, or the Rev. Samuel Harrison, or Harrison Hood, it seems ultimately that the name had a connection, one way or another, to the same original ancestors.

The Harrison community was honored at least once by a visit of Bishop Francis Asbury. In his *Journal* for November 14, 1808, Asbury wrote, "Rode thirty-three miles, hungry, cold, and sick, to Harrison's, Mecklenburg County." Asbury was en route from Lincoln County to Waxhaw, and unfortunately does not mention any activity at Harrison's. [9]

Three other United Methodist churches trace their roots to Harrison—Pineville, Marvin (in Union County), and Pleasant Hill (in Lancaster County), in addition to Hebron Methodist (between Pineville and Charlotte), which no longer exists.

About the time Harrison Church was preparing to erect its first permanent building, another group was forming what would become Mecklenburg's second Methodist society.[10] Inspired by a camp meeting on the Black River in 1814, residents of the Ferrelltown area of northwest Mecklenburg began meeting, probably in the home of a family named Christenbury. First known as "Christenburys," the little society later became "Nazareth" and then "Bethesda."[11] A man named Andrew Moore was among the leaders in the Bethesda group. Bethesda is the name by which the group is most commonly remembered. At some point the group must have erected a wooden building, for Dr. J. B. Alexander refers to it in his book published in 1902, noting, "It is now rotted down."[12]

Today's Asbury United Methodist Church in Huntersville traces its origins to that early congregation known as Bethesda. Asbury Chapel Methodist Episcopal Church officially came into being in August 1865 when Richard Jordan donated two and one half acres of land for a sanctuary, approximately a quarter mile from the site of the present church. According to a church history, it was named for Bishop Francis Asbury.

## Chapter Notes

1. A reference to the founding of Harrison's may be found in *History of Mecklenburg County,* published in 1902 by Dr. J. B. Alexander, p. 267.
2. Albert M. Shipp, *The History of Methodism in South Carolina,* p. 158. Hutchinson's *History of Harrison United Methodist Church,* an unpublished manuscript, is on file with the Commission on Archives and History, Western North Carolina United Methodist Center, and may also be found in the Carolina Room of Public Library of Charlotte and Mecklenburg County.
3. Alexander, p. 267.
4. Charlotte Hastings, in a chapter about Harrison Church in *Our Mecklenburg Heritage,* says on page 54, "He [Hood] became a regular communicant at Harrison Church and may have moved his membership there." However, Orion Hutchinson, on page 14 of his manuscript, writes, "Although he attended the church regularly, it is doubtful that he ever joined the Methodist Church..."
5. Lindsay Pettus, "Heritage Day, Belair Church," an unpublished manuscript obtained from the author, p. 1.
6. *Ibid.*
7. The reference to Harrison's is found in Washington's diary, just before his oft-repeated description of Charlotte as "a trifling place": "Saturday, 28th—Sett off from Crawford's by 4 o'clock and breakfasting at one Harrison's 18 miles. From it got into Charlotte 13 miles further before 3 o'clock." In Volume 6 of *The Diaries of George Washington,* edited by Donald Jackson and Dorothy Twohig, the editors say Washington "...apparently breakfasted with Isaiah Harrison...who lived between McAlpine and Sixmile creeks a short distance southeast of present-day Pineville, N.C." ( Jackson and Twohig, p. 148.) This happens to describe the general location of present-day Harrison United Methodist Church. The 1790 Mecklenburg County census shows an Isaiah Harrison as head of a household that included seven whites and two slaves (p. 383, line 10), but does not indicate his place of residence.
8. Charlotte Hastings, *Our Mecklenburg Heritage,* p. 53.
9. Francis Asbury, *Journal,* Vol. II, p. 582.
10. The chronological narrative in this chapter refers to churches which are in present-day Mecklenburg County. Records at the Western North Carolina Conference Center show that Bethel UMC in Midland was formed in 1790. Elmer T. Clark in his book, *Methodism in Western North Carolina*, states that Bethel dates to an even earlier time, before 1783. At that time, Midland, now in Cabarrus County, was part of Mecklenburg, which would make Bethel at least the second oldest Methodist church in this area. Cabarrus County was created from the eastern section of Mecklenburg in 1792.
11. "Our Heritage," a history of Asbury United Methodist Church, included in the church's *2001 Pictorial Directory.*
12. Alexander, p. 264.

# 7

# David Dunlap

After the Harrison and Bethesda societies were formed, the next surge of Methodist activity would come from another direction, with the arrival in Charlotte of a young man from Waxhaw named David Richardson Dunlap.

David Dunlap is often cited as the "father of Methodism" in Charlotte. Indeed, it would be hard to find a man who did more to plant the seeds of Methodism in the town. And it would be well-nigh impossible to find one with a more colorful story.

Much of what we know of David Dunlap is from the landmark *History of Mecklenburg County* by Dr. J. B. Alexander, published in 1902. More of the Dunlap story is found in the journal of the Rev. James Jenkins, based on an account he received during the annual meeting of the South Carolina Methodist Conference in Charlotte in January 1842. This was within the lifetime of Dr. Dunlap, and it is likely he would have met Jenkins during the conference. Louise Pettus, who has written extensively about the Waxhaw area of Lancaster County, South Carolina, is also a substantial source of information about Dr. Dunlap.

Ironically, Dunlap, the leader of Charlotte's original Methodist congregation, was a grandson of Alexander Craighead, the father of organized Presbyterian worship in Mecklenburg County. Craighead, the fiery pastor to Mecklenburg's early patriots, is considered directly responsible for much of the revolutionary passion that led to the Mecklenburg Declaration of Independence in 1775.

Dunlap's mother was Agnes Nancy Craighead,[1] one of eight children of Alexander Craighead. His father was George Dunlap, member of a prominent family with numerous descendants who still reside in Lancaster County, South Carolina, and Anson County, North Carolina.

George was Agnes' second husband. Her first marriage was to a man who, like her father, was a Presbyterian minister, the Rev. William Richardson.

Richardson had been sent to the Carolinas by the Synod of New York and New Jersey as a missionary to the Cherokees. He installed Alexander Craighead in his first Carolina pastorate at Rocky River in 1758, and later served Providence Presbyterian Church, south of Charlotte. In time, he would become pastor of the Old Waxhaw Church in Lancaster County, South Carolina.

The Old Waxhaw Church was organized in 1755, the same year as Sugaw Creek Church. Only Rocky River, in what is now Cabarrus County, is older. The Waxhaw church nurtured some of the Carolinas' most illustrious figures during its early days, including the parents of future President Andrew Jackson.

The Rev. Richardson was the uncle of William R. Davie, one of North Carolina's most famous patriots and statesmen. Davie was born in England, the son of Archibald and Mary Richardson Davie. About 1764, when William would have been seven or eight years old, the boy, his parents and two other children came to South Carolina. In 1867 Mary Davie died, and William was adopted by Richardson and his new wife, Agnes Craighead. His elders expected young Davie would grow up to be a minister. He attended Queens Museum in Charlotte and graduated from the College of New Jersey (now Princeton) in 1776. But he did not pursue the ministry. Trained as a lawyer, Davie earned distinction as a cavalry officer in the American Revolution, was a North Carolina delegate to the U. S. Constitutional Convention, was elected governor of North Carolina, and founded the University of North Carolina. He was appointed a brigadier general in the U. S. Army by President John Adams in 1798. Davie died in 1820 and is buried at the Old Waxhaw Church.

Richardson and Agnes had no children of their own, which may be just as well, for tragedy would soon strike. In 1771, a dozen years

*David Richardson Dunlap*

into their marriage, Richardson died under mysterious circumstances. According to the story, recorded in the archives of Old Waxhaw Church, he was found in his study with a horse's bridle around his neck, apparently a suicide. But when Agnes remarried a year after his death, suspicions arose about the circumstances of his demise. The body was dug from the grave and church members conducted an ancient Scottish ritual called "trial by touch." Agnes was forced to place her fingers on the forehead of the corpse. According to the old Scottish tradition, if her fingers bled, she was guilty of murder. Fortunately for Agnes, there was no blood. Archibald Richardson, brother-in-law of the deceased, pressed her fingers against the forehead, so much so that she cried out in pain. But still there was no blood. It was concluded that Agnes was innocent of her husband's death.[2]

Agnes' new husband was Captain George Dunlap. Some sources say Captain Dunlap was from Wadesboro, and he did appear to have relatives there. However, the Dunlap family was well established in the Waxhaw area, and the couple evidently retained their ties to the Old Waxhaw church.

George and Agnes had five children. The second-born of the five was a son, named David Richardson Dunlap. Calculating from information on Dunlap's tombstone, the birth date was October 6, 1777. Evidently choosing to honor her first husband, Agnes used his surname, Richardson, as the middle name for her son.

Nothing is known of Dunlap's early life. We know that his mother died November 9, 1790, when David was 13 years old. His father, Captain George Dunlap, lived another ten years, dying at the age of 64.[3] Both parents are thought to be buried at the Old Waxhaw Church cemetery, although the graves are unmarked. Monuments memorializing the couple were placed at the cemetery by family descendants now living in Ansonville, North Carolina.

In May 1802 an interdenominational camp meeting was held near the Old Waxhaw church, led by Presbyterian, Methodist, and Baptist preachers. Different accounts list the number attending as anywhere from three to six thousand spirited worshippers. In all likelihood David was an eager participant in the revival, and found his soul moved by the exuberant worship of Methodists amid the throng. David was not the only one moved. Despite the cooperative mood displayed by the revival, Presbyterian eyebrows were raised when the pastor of Old Waxhaw Church, Rev. John Brown, was seen taking communion with the Methodists. Contributing to Brown's fall from favor was his effort to introduce Methodist hymns to his Presbyterian services. Soon thereafter Brown relocated to Wadesboro, where he accepted the leadership of a high school. In her book, *The Waxhaws*, Louise Pettus reports that Rev. Brown took David Dunlap with him. David would have been about 25 years old.

Dunlap's years in Anson County have been difficult to trace, but several events have been pieced together from various sources. It was during this time that he took up the practice of medicine, perhaps as an understudy to an established physician.[4] It would be a career he would pursue for some 40 years.

It was also during this time that he first became a husband and father. From genealogical records it appears he was first married about 1804 to Elizabeth Jennings, a daughter of John and Elizabeth Lanier Jennings of Anson County. In 1807 they had a son, George Hamilton Dunlap, known as Hamilton, who later moved to Alabama. A marker at Settlers Cemetery in Charlotte indicates that David and Elizabeth also had another son, John, who died in 1838. He is buried next to his father in Charlotte, along with other members of Dunlap's family.[5]

Not too many years into the marriage Elizabeth Dunlap died, and Dunlap married her sister, Charlotte Jennings. David and Charlotte had one son, Edmund. According to the burial inscription in Settlers Cemetery, Charlotte died in October 1815, about the time Edmund was born, suggesting she may have died in childbirth or almost immediately thereafter. Edmund died less than eight months after his mother.[6]

David Dunlap then wed a third time, to Mary Jane "Polly" Lowrie, a daughter of the prominent Mecklenburg legislator and judge, Samuel Lowrie. One of Polly's sisters, Lillie, was married to another Charlotte political and civic leader, Brawley Oates. Later, Brawley Oates and David Dunlap would serve together on the town council. The Oates family was also active in the new Methodist congregation in Charlotte. Both Polly and Lillie would later be members of the first "Ladies Aid Society" organized in Charlotte, forerunner of today's United Methodist Women.[7]

The fact that Dunlap, product of a Presbyterian dynasty, could become a towering figure in local Methodism may seem odd at first. It is all the more so since Methodists were held in low esteem in those days by their Presbyterian neighbors.

It was while Dunlap was in Anson County that he became a confirmed Methodist. The reasons are clouded in history. Perhaps he was influenced by the Waxhaw camp meeting of 1802, or other Methodist revivals which were common during the period.

Historian J. B. Alexander tells another, more colorful story of Dunlap's conversion. In Alexander's account, Dunlap's second marriage, to Charlotte, a sister of his first wife, was a violation of Presbyterian rules of that day, and he was expelled from the church. As of this writing we have been unable to document Alexander's account. However, we do know that there were "prohibited degrees of relationship" within which a faithful Presbyterian could not marry, and in October 1799 the Presbyterian Synod of the Carolinas, meeting at Hopewell Church, considered one case specifically dealing with a man who had married his former wife's sister, "and had with her been under suspension for some time..." The persons involved in that case are not identified, but it does give credence to the possibility that Dunlap was cast out for that offense.

Whatever the reason for Dunlap's new allegiance, the Presbyterian loss was a Methodist gain, for Dunlap was to become a leading supporter of John Wesley's young movement. He would become founder or active supporter in the establishment of at least three Methodist churches, and probably more. One may have been Concord Methodist, organized in Ansonville in 1808. He apparently was also the class leader of a society organized by the Rev. John Schrock in Wadesboro in 1812. In an 1846 article in *The Southern Christian Advocate*, "Methodism in Anson County," Samuel Leard recounts that Schrock "raised a society" of about 60 members who were placed under the charge of a Dr. Dunlap, "...of whose pious labors as a class leader grateful recollections are still retained among some of the older members."

In April 1814, two months after his second marriage, David Dunlap moved to Charlotte. Jenkins relates that Dunlap passed through Charlotte one day, looking for a place to establish a medical practice, and called on a first cousin, Samuel Craighead Caldwell. Caldwell was the son of Rachel Craighead Caldwell and her husband, the Rev. David Caldwell of Guilford County. He was the pastor of three Presbyterian churches, and undoubtedly was the area's foremost religious leader at that time. Caldwell urged his cousin to move to Charlotte, no doubt considering the prospect of having another good doctor in town. The two men joked that Dunlap might also promote Methodism as well as medicine in Mecklenburg, a prospect that turned out to be no joke at all for either man.

At the time Dunlap arrived in Charlotte, the community now called "the city of churches" had no church at all. The Charlotte city limits extended less than a mile in any direction from a brick courthouse, recently completed on the site of the original log courthouse in the square. The nearest church building was Sugaw Creek Presbyterian, some four miles north on the Salisbury Road, a rural extension of downtown's Tryon Street. Residents closer to Charlotte's crossroads had attended religious meetings at times under the trees behind a blacksmith shop where First Presbyterian Church is now located. The town's original burying ground, Settlers Cemetery, was started in 1776 in the adjoining block.

"Indoor" worship services were often held at the courthouse.

Methodist churches existed during that time, but none within convenient traveling distance from Charlotte. Bethel Church at Midland, in what is now Cabarrus County, had been started by 1790, perhaps earlier. A group which would become Harrison (or Harrison's) Methodist had been organized in 1785, meeting in a brush arbor south of Pineville on the road to Lancaster. Their first building was erected about 1815. Buckhill, now Trinity Methodist, north of Charlotte on Beatties Ford Road, also dates its existence from 1815.

David Dunlap is credited with having a hand in the formation of Buckhill Church. Margaret Kerr Martin, a widow and former Presbyterian, began holding prayer services in her home after a meeting with Dunlap. It seems likely that traveling Methodist ministers who found their way to Mrs. Martin's home were steered there by Dunlap. The society formed in the Martin home eventually became the Buckhill Church.

During this same time, Dr. Dunlap was inviting Methodist preachers to include Charlotte in their travels. Among these was a close friend, the Rev. William Terry of Fayetteville. Services were usually held at the courthouse.

In his journal the Rev. James Jenkins tells the story that one of those Methodist meetings was interrupted when Dunlap's cousin, the Rev. Samuel Caldwell, who had previously urged Dunlap to move to Charlotte, arrived with some of his Presbyterian followers and

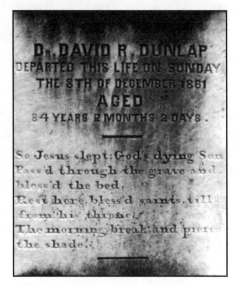

*Monument to David Dunlap in Settlers Cemetery. The
monument bears the inscription shown on the right.*

began preaching about the shortcomings of Methodist beliefs. Jenkins
relates that, when Caldwell departed, the Methodist preacher, William
Barnett, resumed his service. As Jenkins describes it:

> After a short time Mr. Barnett took the stage, and observed to the people,
> that they no doubt expected a reply to brother C.'s observations
> respecting the Methodists; in this they should be disappointed: his
> business was to preach the gospel for the salvation of sinners, and not
> to make proselytes. And [he] observed further, that if any person wished
> to know the doctrines and usages of the Methodist Church, their books
> were abroad in the land; could be easily procured, and examined
> deliberately at their leisure. In his first prayer he appeared fervently to
> pray, that the preceding labours of the day by brother C., so far as
> consistent with God's word and will, should be sanctified to the good
> of those who heard.  This being done, he preached a very excellent
> gospel sermon, on Acts x, 34, 35, to a deeply attentive congregation.

Jenkins says that the Reverend Caldwell urged his followers to
boycott Dr. Dunlap's medical practice, nearly wiping out Dunlap

financially. For all of this, Caldwell was roundly criticized by his own members, and, according to Jenkins, would have been dismissed from his congregations had a few of his friends not interceded. It is interesting, however, to note an entirely different perspective on Rev. Caldwell's demeanor, as related by the Presbyterian writer, Rev. William Henry Foote:

> And when he was harshly charged, because he would not yield his own pulpit and his long accustomed hour of preaching to his people, for the purpose of permitting efforts to be made to divide his congregation, the perfect coolness and unwavering resolution with which he met the assault, tempered the storm to a harmless breeze. He had enough of the cool and calm resolution of his father, David Caldwell, of Guilford, the sixth minister in Carolina, to make him immoveable, when he felt convinced; and enough of the warm heart and ardent piety of his mother, the daughter of Craighead, to make him both lovely and beloved.

In later years, Rev. Caldwell was afflicted with severe rheumatism and called on Dunlap for assistance. In Jenkins' account, Caldwell complained that he had been "rolling and tossing all night like a wild bull in a net, and wondering what object the Lord could have in view of afflicting me so severely..." Perhaps, Caldwell supposed, the Lord wanted to teach him patience.

Dunlap responded, "If the Lord had brought him so far on the list, he would carry him through before he was done with him." The doctor explained he was thinking of the book of Second Peter, where a list of virtues includes patience, as well as others.[8] Caldwell, says Jenkins, "at once saw the bearing, and felt its force." Thereupon, the two men made their peace.

Dunlap's espousal of Methodism evidently caused quite a strain with others in his family. Among these was a man identified in Alexander's book as Dr. D. T. Caldwell. This was likely David Thomas Caldwell, a son of the Rev. Samuel Caldwell, who was, like Dunlap, a physician. Alexander says Dr. Caldwell and Dunlap had not spoken for years, until Caldwell's son died. (There is a grave in Settlers Cemetery identified as that of Samuel Craighead Caldwell, son of D. T. Caldwell, who died in 1844 at the age of 17.) Dr. Dunlap visited Caldwell to express his condolences. "Dr. Caldwell met him at the door, both shed tears of reconciliation, forgot the past, and were the best of friends in future life."[9]

In the latter part of 1818, according to Jenkins, the first Methodist "class" was organized in Charlotte with Dr. Dunlap as leader. At first they probably met in the courthouse, later using the new town church erected by local government in the second block of West Trade Street.

In 1835, unable to pay off a note on the church, the town council voted to sell it to John Irwin, a leading member of the Presbyterian congregation. David Dunlap was one of the town commissioners who signed the deed.

In 1832, with the original town church destined to become exclusively Presbyterian, the Methodists constructed their first church building at College and Seventh Streets, where the First United Presbyterian Church is now located. In 1859 a new edifice was constructed at Tryon and Sixth Streets, and the name became Tryon Street Methodist. This church later merged with Trinity Methodist (the one in downtown Charlotte, not on Beatties Ford Road) to become what is now First United Methodist Church.

During his illustrious career as a church layman, Dunlap served as a trustee for the Methodist Circuit and was active in Methodist affairs countywide. Alexander reports that Dunlap was also a clerk and master of the Court of Equity for many years. He is listed in old city records as a town commissioner for at least two terms.

In addition to his other famous relatives, Dunlap had an indirect link with South Carolina politician and U. S. Vice President John C. Calhoun. Calhoun was born to the second wife of Patrick Calhoun, whose first wife, Jane Craighead, was Dunlap's maternal aunt.

Dunlap's wife Polly died on May 19, 1848 at the age of 56. Their daughter, Harriet, first married to Dr. Edmund Jones, of Morganton, later became the second wife of Col. Thomas H. Brem about 1858.[8] Brem was a prominent Charlotte merchant, and held his officer's rank from service in the Civil War. His son by his first marriage, Walter Brem, grew up to be a prominent Charlotte insurance executive in the early 1900s.

Dr. Dunlap lived out his final years with his daughter, and died on Sunday, December 8, 1861, "aged 84 years, 2 months, 2 days" as inscribed on his tombstone.

He and Polly were laid to rest in the center of Settler's Cemetery, under a striking obelisk monument, the tallest in the graveyard, erected by his children. It bears the following inscription:

> So Jesus slept: God's dying Son
> Pass'd through the grave and
> bless'd the bed.
> Rest here, bless'd saints, till
> from His throne,
> The morning break and pierce the shade.

# Chapter Notes

1.  Her full maiden name was either Agnes Nancy Craighead or Nancy Agnes Craighead. Sources disagree on this point. Most accounts refer to her as Nancy, but she is called "Agnes" in her father's will, and the name Agnes is on a memorial marker at the Old Waxhaw Presbyterian Church cemetery in Lancaster County.
2.  Marquis James, *The Life of Andrew Jackson*, p. 9. The story is also reported by Louise Pettus in *The Waxhaws.*
3.  Dates of death are from markers in the Old Waxhaw Presbyterian Church Cemetery.
4.  Limited research did not disclose how Dr. Dunlap received his medical training. Dr. Francis Kron, who practiced medicine in Stanly County, has been described as the first formally trained physician to work in the southern Piedmont. He arrived in Stanly County about 1834.
5.  Members of Dunlap's family buried in Settlers Cemetery are listed on a marker at the grave site. The complete text of the marker is difficult to read, but it has been transcribed by the Mecklenburg Historical Association as follows:
    These walls contain the remains of Dr. D. R. Dunlap's family / 1st Charlotte Dunlap died 25th October 1815 aged about 24 years / 2nd Edmund Dunlap their son died 21st June 1816 aged 7 months / 3rd Wm S. Dunlap died 31st October 1820 aged 8 months / 4th Margaret Dunlap died 7th August 1823 aged __years / 5th Mary Agness Dunlap died __ May 1833 aged __years / the last ___ were children of Mary & D. R. Dunlap / 6th John Dunlap son by 1st marriage died 16th August 1838 / 7th Mary Dunlap last ___of D.R.D. died 19th May 1848 aged 56 years.
6.  Conclusion based on the inscription above.
7.  Mildred Morse McEwen, p. 110.
8.  Second Peter 1:5-6, "...add to your faith virtue, and to virtue knowledge; and to knowledge temperance; and to temperance patience; and to patience godliness." KJV
9.  J. B. Alexander, *History of Mecklenburg County,* p. 179.

# 8

# "Rural Trinity"

In 19th century Piedmont Carolina the Methodists and Presbyterians had a strange relationship. The Presbyterians had arrived first and were unchallenged as the dominant faith for many years. But as the evangelistic revival of the "New Awakening" spread across America around 1800, coinciding with the arrival of circuit-riding Methodist preachers, Presbyterians often found themselves working alongside Methodists at camp meetings, and even occasionally opened the doors of their churches for Methodist preaching. Francis Asbury spoke warmly of the hospitality he'd had with Presbyterians.

But at times relations were less than friendly. One reason might have been that some Presbyterian ministers simply saw the Methodists as johnny-come-lately competitors. To some, the Methodists represented an English church, and the Scots-Irish Presbyterians were never especially fond of the English. There were accusations that Methodists indulged unqualified preachers. And the fact that Methodists found receptive converts among the poor and uneducated did not help their social standing.[1]

There was also a theological difference, though it was probably exaggerated by overly serious clergy on both sides. The issue was predestination, or, as the Presbyterians more often described it, election and reprobation. From the Presbyterian perspective, Methodists, with their belief in universal redemption, were seriously misguided and were leading seekers astray.

In many Presbyterian congregations the faithful were told to stay away from Methodist gatherings. Transgressors could be denied the sacraments of the church, or even expelled from membership.

*Betty Moore· 1968*

*Trinity's First Building—This drawing, by former Trinity Church member Betty Moore (now Mrs. Betty Moore Hafter), is a log building similar to the first church building in 1815. The drawing appears on the cover of a book on the history of Trinity Church. Used by permission of Mrs. Hafter.*

One such transgressor was the recently widowed Margaret Kerr Martin, who lived with her seven children in the bounds of the Hopewell Church in northern Mecklenburg County. She and some others had gone to a camp meeting conducted by the Rev. W. C. Davies, himself a former Presbyterian. For this, they were cast out from the Presbyterian fold.[2]

Finding herself without a church to attend, she traveled to Charlotte to call upon David Dunlap, who had gained attention by inviting Methodist preachers to speak in Charlotte. She spent the night at Dunlap's home, eagerly learning about the Methodist faith. The doctor promised to lead prayer meetings at Mrs. Kerr's home.

Not long thereafter Mrs. Martin entertained another visitor, the Rev. Samuel Harrison. After spending a night he agreed to return in three weeks to lead a worship service.

As a history of Trinity Church relates, "Upon the appointed evening the house and yard were filled with people who welcomed the preacher as he arrived at sundown. After silent prayer, Mr. Harrison sang a hymn alone."

Mrs. Martin's son, William, later wrote, "Oh! What singing! It was new; the people were amazed."

At the end of the service Rev. Harrison offered to come again three weeks hence, an offer which was warmly received. On the next visit Rev. Harrison was accompanied by the Rev. William Barnett, soon to be named presiding elder of the Sugar Creek Circuit. A Methodist society was organized. The home became a regular preaching place which was simply called "Martin's."

Within a year it was decided to build a meeting house.[3] A site was selected on Margaret Kerr's land, on a bluff called Buckhill[4] about a mile from the present Trinity Church. A nearby spring was called Buck Spring. The names referred to deer, often seen in the area. Neighbors brought their tools and erected a log structure covered with clapboards. The boards had been cut in a nearby water-powered sawmill owned by an uncle, John Kerr, who happened to be a Presbyterian. The church took its name from its location and remained at that site until 1833.

On September 30, 1833 a new L-shaped building was dedicated at the site of the present church. It seated about 100 worshippers, including space in a slave gallery. With the new building the church acquired a new name, Trinity. Later it would be known unofficially as "rural Trinity" to distinguish it from the "Charlotte Trinity" established in 1896.

Among the trustees in 1833 was Brawley Oates, brother-in-law of Dr. David Dunlap.

The current sanctuary of Trinity Church was completed in 1928. According to the church history, a faithful member, Mrs. Rose Elliott, started a fund for the new sanctuary by donating 25 cents at a quilting party.

William Martin was eight years old when the first log church was built, and his writings provide much of the early history of the church. He later became a Methodist preacher himself, admitted on trial to the South Carolina Conference in January 1828, at the age of

21. He gave his first sermon in the log church after being licensed to preach. Little is known of the other Martin children. Mrs. Martin remarried in 1812 to a local Methodist preacher named Robert Tucker, and the family moved across the river into Lincoln County.

It appears that Dr. David Dunlap took an active role in the formative years of the new Buckhill Church. He was listed as a class leader among "members present" at a meeting of the Sugar Creek Circuit on May 25, 1816. This was two years before the date when, according to Jenkins, Dunlap formed a class in Charlotte. On July 27, 1816, he was appointed a steward of the circuit. Exactly when Dunlap made the transition to class leader in Charlotte is not clear, since the quarterly conference minutes show Charlotte as a preaching place as early as 1815.[5]

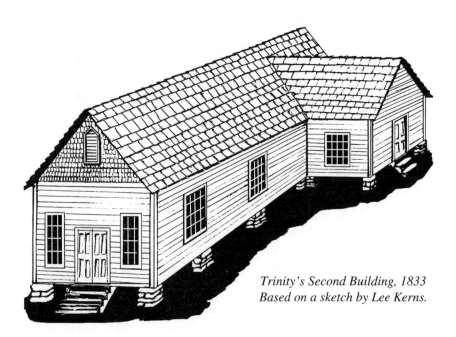

*Trinity's Second Building, 1833
Based on a sketch by Lee Kerns.*

# Chapter Notes

1. J. B. Alexander, *History of Mecklenburg County,* p. 264
2. Except where noted otherwise, the balance of this narrative is based on *The History of Trinity Methodist Church,* published by the Historical Committee, July 15, 1968.
3. The earliest buildings erected for worship by Methodists were not called churches,. They were called "meeting houses." Instead of saying "I am going to church," one would say, "I am going to meeting." No doubt this was the origin of the expression "Sunday go-to-meeting clothes."
4. Some writers render the name as "Buck Hill." However, in the church's own history, as well as in minutes of the Sugar Creek Circuit, it is called "Buckhill" (one word).
5. Minutes of quarterly meetings of the Sugar Creek Circuit, on file with the Commission on Archives and History, United Methodist Center.

# 9

# The Town Church

From the time of its first settlement in the 1750s until the early years of the 1800s, the town of Charlotte had never had a church building. Sugaw Creek Church, established in 1755 some three and one half miles north of town, served the Presbyterian families who lived in the Charlottetown community. From time to time, ministers from Sugaw Creek preached in Charlotte, usually at the courthouse in the Square, built in 1767.

About 1815, town commissioners decided to build a nondenominational community church to be used by all faiths. (Various dates are cited by different sources. The year 1815 is used in a history of First Presbyterian Church, which has extensive records relating to these events. Taking the various sources into account, a plausible conclusion would be that the decision by town officials was made several years before the land was acquired or construction began.) According to some traditions, it was David Dunlap and his fledgling class of Methodists who inspired and campaigned for the town church, because of their own need for a place of worship.[1]

The second block of West Trade Street was selected as the site. The sequence of events surrounding this choice is not clear. Most written histories imply that the site for the church and the adjoining cemetery, now known as Settlers Cemetery, were chosen at the same time, when the town fathers decided to build the community church. This does not, however, agree with other known facts.

The first burial in Settlers Cemetery was in 1776, suggesting that this place had already been set aside for the purpose. And the site of what is now First Presbyterian Church had apparently been regarded as a gathering place for worship for many years. The Presbyterian minister John Thomson, who settled in what is now lower Iredell County in 1751, may have preached in the grove of trees where First Presbyterian Church now stands as early as 1752.[2]

On March 22, 1772, two lots in Block 19, the block where First Presbyterian Church now stands, were deeded by town commissioners to Waightstill Avery. A second deed is recorded in 1774, similar to the 1772 deed. The circumstances or purpose are not clear. It is assumed the property reverted to town ownership at some point, perhaps because nothing was built on it, as required.

By 1805 the Rev. Samuel C. Caldwell of Sugaw Creek was preaching once each month in Charlotte. The location was not recorded, but again we assume it was in the courthouse. Records indicate he continued until 1826, by which time the new Town Church had been completed.

In 1817 William Davidson purchased five lots in block 19 for $34.25. Two years later he deeded the lots to the town for $125 for "a church now building." This indicates the church was already under construction. Other records refer to a "brick church." John Irwin, who will figure prominently in the story as it unfolds, was one of the town commissioners at the time of this transaction.[3]

The brick structure was completed in 1823. Already the Presbyterians were ready to use it. A Charlotte congregation had been recognized by the Concord Presbytery in September 1821. It was formally organized on the fourth Sunday in August 1832.

The Brick Church must have been a busy place. In addition to the Presbyterians, David Dunlap's Methodist group began using the building. St. Peters Episcopal Church, organized in 1834, held their worship services there before moving to their present site at Tryon and Seventh Streets. Records indicate that a Baptist group also used the Brick Church.

Meanwhile, the town commissioners were having financial difficulties involving the church. Originally they had hoped construction could be financed with contributions from groups that used the building, but donations had been slow in coming. The town had borrowed $1,500 from the Charlotte branch of the Bank of New Bern to finish the building. But when the note became due in 1835 with a balance of $674 still on the books, the town fathers voted to sell the Brick Church. John Irwin, a town commissioner[4] and a leading member of the Presbyterian congregation, paid off the note, and received the deed to the property. Within a few years he was reimbursed by his fellow church members, and, on March 24, 1841, he signed the deed over to them. The cemetery was not included in the transfer, and is still owned and maintained by the city.

The original Brick Church no longer stands. The oldest existing structure now on the property was erected in 1857. The facade of that building, to which the steeple was later added, is the central part of the church complex we see today.

As the conversion of Town Church to Presbyterian Church was unfolding, the Methodists had already been looking for a place of worship they could call their own. In 1832 they moved into a new church they had built at Seventh and College Streets, where the First United Presbyterian Church now stands.

## Chapter Notes

1. Some sources say that Dr. Dunlap was a member of the town council at this time. However, his name does not among members for that year as listed in the City Code. Also, if the date of Dr. Dunlap's moving to Charlotte, 1814, is correct, it is unlikely he would have held elective office the very next year.

2. Blythe, LeGette and Charles Brockmann, *Hornets' Nest, The Story of Charlotte and Mecklenburg County,* p. 20.

3. Unofficial Appendix to Code of the City of Charlotte, 1887, p. 243.

4. John Irwin is listed in town records as a commissioner in 1835, but sometime during the year he resigned. It is not clear if he resigned before he paid off the note to acquire the property, although he could have done so to avoid a conflict of interest.

# 10

# Four Wards,
# Four Churches

David Dunlap's original Methodist "class" in Charlotte probably held its earliest meetings in the county courthouse, which at that time was still located at the intersection of Trade and Tryon Streets, known locally as "the Square."[1] Later they worshipped in the Town Church, also known as the "Brick Church," on the site of present-day First Presbyterian Church.

There is evidence that another building also served as a Methodist church in the 1820s. Quarterly Conference minutes of the Sugar Creek Circuit from April 20, 1822, say five trustees, one of whom was Dr. Dunlap, were appointed to build a church in Charlotte. There is no further reference to this committee, or the church building, in minutes after this date. In his memoirs, the Rev. James Jenkins comments that soon after Dr. Dunlap formed the Charlotte society in 1818, "...it was attempted to build a house of worship, and though the building was not entirely completed, it served as a place of worship for a number of years."[2] In Mildred McEwen's history of First United Methodist Church, she quotes an advertisement in the Catawba Journal of December 15, 1824, which refers to some lots for sale "adjoining the Methodist Church."[3]

Except for these sketchy references, the existence of such a church has not been confirmed. However, another bit of tantalizing evidence may be relevant. Records in the Mecklenburg County Register of Deeds office indicate that the Charlotte Circuit, Methodist Episcopal Church South, had, at some time before 1860, acquired land at Fifth and Brevard Streets. The lot, about a quarter acre in size, was on the northeast corner of Fifth and Brevard, now part of the site of Charlotte's new uptown arena. Records say church trustees had pledged the land for a debt, and when they failed to pay off the debt, it was sold at public auction in December 1860 to E. E. Black of Cabarrus County. The names of the Methodist trustees are difficult to read, but appear to be W. Still, J. W. Martin, Wm. A. Ardry and Sampson Wolf. There was a J. W. Martin at rural Trinity Church during this time. There was a William A. Ardrey at Tryon Street. As mentioned, there is no record of a church being located at Fifth and Brevard, and the deed does not refer to a building on the property. The circumstances surrounding it are unexplained. It could have been the site of an old Methodist meeting place. Or perhaps the property had been acquired as a potential new church site before the Tryon Street Church was built.

The first documented Methodist church building in Charlotte was at the corner of College and Seventh Streets. Tradition says it was built in 1832, although the deed to the property is dated January 5, 1833.[4] The property was purchased from the Town of Charlotte. Among the five town commissioners who signed for the town was Brawley Oates, who was, coincidentally, a member of the Methodist congregation. David R. Dunlap was one of the Methodist trustees named as purchasers. According to the deed, the Methodists acquired two lots, together fronting the entire length of College Street from Seventh to Eighth Streets. However, when the property was sold to St. Mark's Lutheran Church a quarter century later, only the lot at College and Seventh was mentioned. The disposition of the other lot has not been traced.[5]

The building at College and Seventh would serve the small but growing congregation for the next 27 years. During this time it was apparently known in Methodist circles only as "Charlotte" or "Charlotte Station." Records in the Mecklenburg County Register of Deeds Office refer to it simply as the "M E Church South."

Its successor, Tryon Street Church, at the corner of Sixth and Tryon on the edge of Fourth Ward where the Dunhill Hotel now stands, was finished in 1859. In a roster of charter members of the new Tryon Street church, Dr. Dunlap is listed as a steward of "Charlotte Station" along with E. H. Andrews, Charles Wilson, T. J. Holton, E. A. Yates and R. W. Beckwith. Dunlap's son-in-law, Col. Thomas Brem, was a member of the Building Committee, which

*Tryon Street M. E. Church, South*
*This view shows a three-arch portico across the front between the two towers*
*which is not seen in earlier photos. This was added as part of a remodeling*
*project in 1908. The church had been rebuilt in 1891, but the front part, having*
*been renovated just seven years previously, was preserved.*
*From the collection of Mary Manning Boyer*

also included E. H. Andrews and James Sanders. Harriet Brem, daughter of David Dunlap and wife of Thomas Brem, was a charter member.[6]

The cornerstone for the new Tryon Street Church was laid August 17, 1859 in a ceremony conducted by Phalanx Lodge of the Masonic Fraternity. The original building was replaced in 1891, saving only the facade of the earlier structure. Probably the most striking feature of the Tryon Street church was its slender, soaring steeple, towering above the Charlotte skyline. The steeple is clearly visible in numerous old photos of downtown Charlotte from the period.

Ironically, just as the Methodists were about to vacate their old building at Seventh and College, Charlotte's first Lutheran congregation was forming and needed a place of worship. Pastor G. D. Bernheim, minister of Old St. John's Lutheran Church in Cabarrus County and head of the struggling Mount Pleasant College, came to Charlotte in January 1859 to raise funds for the college. However, responding to public interest, he ended up organizing a church instead. The story of what happened next is recounted in a history of St. Mark's Evangelical Lutheran Church, written by Charlotte attorney Phillip Gerdes:

> Pastor Bernheim reports that in short order he had about $600 to start the new enterprise, bartered for the old Episcopal Church building, located on Trade Street, opposite the United States Mint (now the Federal Court House Building). Later on the trustees of the congregation changed their minds and purchased the old Methodist Church on the corner of Seventh and College Streets for $600; they, the Methodists, reserving the right to worship in it every two weeks, when not in use by the Lutherans, until their new church edifice on Tryon Street was finished.[7]

The Lutherans later moved to a new sanctuary on North Tryon Street, and in February 1773 the property at Seventh and College was acquired by predecessors of what is now the First United Presbyterian Church.[8] It is interesting to note that the building erected first as home of Charlotte's original Methodist congregation would also be the home of its original Lutheran congregation, and the site would later be used by one of the city's original African American congregations.

Not long after the new Tryon Street Methodist Church was finished the congregation agreed to sacrifice the bell from their tower for the Civil War effort. *The Western Democrat* [newspaper] of May 6, 1862, carried the following article on page 3:

> The Methodist, Episcopal, Baptist and Lutheran churches having given their bells to the government for the purpose of being cast into cannon, they were removed last week and broken up for shipment to Richmond, where a battery of guns will be immediately prepared for Capt. Brem of this place. We have been furnished with the weight of the bells as follows: Methodist, 1583 lbs., Episcopal, 298, Baptist, 137, Lutheran, 120—Total 2138 lbs."[9]

If the weights are correct, the Methodist bell was substantially larger than the others. It is noteworthy that the bell from the Presbyterian Church (now First Presbyterian) is not mentioned. According to tradition, when the call came for bells to be melted down in the war effort, the town was to keep its courthouse bell. Because of the historic value attached to the Presbyterian bell, it was decided to save it and send the courthouse bell instead.

Oddly, however, according to a newspaper account in the *Daily Charlotte Observer* of April 29, 1873, the Presbyterian bell was not moved to the courthouse, but to the Methodist church instead. The article is about a new bell being installed in the Presbyterian church, and adds:

> The old bell of the Presbyterian Church is now used for the Town clock in the steeple of the Methodist Church, where it was placed during the war. It was the only church bell in the city that was not sacrificed for the Confederate cause.

A Presbyterian version does not mention the bell ever being in the Methodist church, saying only that it was placed in the courthouse, where it rang for many years to announce church services, sessions of court, and fires. Later it was moved to First Ward School, where it

*Businessman B. D. Heath...*          *The Rev. John F. Butt, a founder of*
*Provided land for churches.*          *Calvary and Dilworth churches.*

remained until 1943. At that time it was returned to the Presbyterians, where it is now preserved as a historic treasure.[10]

One of the most often-repeated stories from the days of Tryon Street Church is that it was here on November 30, 1885, that Charles J. Soong was ordained a Methodist minister. The Rev. Soong was the father of the Soong sisters, one of whom became Madame Chiang Kai-shek and the other, the wife of Sun Yat Sen.[11]

Following establishment of Mecklenburg's first churches, Methodism expanded rapidly across the county. Zion (now Mt. Zion) was started in 1827. Hickory Grove (then known as Prospect) was founded in 1844. Zoar came in 1861,[12] followed by Calvary in 1865.

Calvary was the second Methodist church to be started in what we now call "uptown," and it moved several times. It began as a mission effort of Tryon Street Church under the leadership of the Rev. John F. Butt.[13] Its first location was on South Mint Street. A deed dated May 29, 1896, shows the trustees of "Church Street

Church, formerly known as Church Street Chapel," purchased a tract of land on South Church Street. Church trustees mentioned in the deed are G. M. Holobaugh, J. J. Shuman, J. W. Tyzzer, George J. Etheridge and R. E. Holder. The land is described as being between Church and Poplar Streets in Third Ward, and apparently adjoining some land the church already owned. Available records make it difficult to pinpoint the exact location. However, we know from city directories that by 1915 the church was on South Church Street in Third Ward, on part of the block now occupied by a Charlotte Observer parking deck. The minister of Calvary Church, the Rev. Robert S. Howie, lived next door at 616 South Church Street. In 1934 Calvary moved again, to 1301 South Mint Street near its original location, and in 1952 moved to its present home at 512 West Boulevard.

1866 saw the official beginning of Big Spring Church, the outgrowth of a camp meeting which had started years earlier; and Simpson Chapel, which would later become part of today's Simpson-Gillespie UMC. Pineville Church got its start in 1867 as a cooperative effort with a new Presbyterian congregation. The two churches shared meeting space in a school, and later in a building erected by the Presbyterians. Pineville became an official appointment on a Methodist circuit in 1878.

Matthews Methodist was started in 1877 by 20 members of a church in nearby Union County. Seversville (later Wesley Heights) was organized in 1883, followed by Moore's Chapel (an outgrowth of Dow's) in 1884.

In 1888 the congregation of Tryon Street Church organized a new mission church which would become Brevard Street Methodist Episcopal Church.[14] A committee from Tryon Street including M. F. Kirby, Mrs. W. F. Bennett and Miss Lou Vogler conducted services. Anna Bobbington Dowd was the organist.

From the beginning the mission was a success. Within a few years the congregation became too large for the small house and, about 1894, a lot was acquired on North Brevard Street, between 11th and 12th Streets. A wooden building was erected, but it, too, was soon outgrown. A new site was purchased at 614 North Brevard Street and in 1898 a Sunday School building was constructed. A house next door at 612 North Brevard was the parsonage. In 1905 the main church building was finished, and the name became Brevard Street Methodist Episcopal Church. In 1954 the church moved to a new building at its present location on Central Avenue, and changed its name to Memorial Methodist Church.

1888 was also the year that Oak Grove and Pleasant Grove were begun. Derita Methodist, later renamed Cole Memorial in honor of the Rev. E. O. Cole, was organized in 1891 (some records say 1890).

As the 19th century drew to a close uptown Charlotte had three Methodist churches located in First, Third and Fourth Wards. Whether or not by design, the next to be organized would be in Second Ward, giving each ward its own Methodist house of worship.

Trinity Methodist Church was organized in 1896 as an offshoot of Tryon Street Church when the original congregation grew so large that the division seemed desirable. "Charlotte Trinity," as it has been called to distinguish it from the older "Rural Trinity" on Beatties Ford Road, was built at Second and Tryon Streets, where Three Wachovia Center is now located. Many will remember this as the site, for many years, of another landmark, the Charlotte Branch of the Federal Reserve Bank.

Quarterly Conference minutes of Tryon Street Church from January 7, 1896, list 113 members who transferred to the new Trinity Church. In all, according to other records, 500 people left Tryon Street to form the Trinity congregation.[15]

Land for Trinity was purchased by trustees of Tryon Street Church from M. P. Pegram on August 1, 1895, and transferred to the trustees of the new church April 8, 1898. The price for the property, identified as lot 181 on a map of Charlotte, was six thousand, three hundred dollars. The deed notes that the purchase was authorized by

*Trinity M. E. Church, South*
*From the collection of Mary Manning Boyer*

the Quarterly Conference of Tryon Street Methodist Episcopal Church South.

An overlap appears in the names of trustees of the two churches. In the transfer of ownership from Tryon Street to Trinity, M. L. Mayer and R. N. Littlejohn, trustees, "parties of the first part," are also listed among trustees of Trinity Methodist Episcopal Church South, as "parties of the second part."

In 1891, businessman Edward D. Latta unveiled his plans for Charlotte's first streetcar suburb, to which he applied his middle name,

Dilworth. Latta's ambitious plans were boosted when D. A. Tompkins, owner of Atherton Mill, bought an entire block to build mill houses for workers.

The area was ripe for church extension. According to tradition, the Rev. John F. Butt, who previously helped start Calvary Church, built the first Methodist church in Dilworth, a small wooden structure, with his own funds.[16]

In March 1896, M. C. Mayer, Walter Brem, D. M. Rigler, M. L. Frazier and R. N. Littlejohn, formerly of Tryon Street Church but acting as trustees of Trinity Church, purchased a lot at Cleveland and Worthington Avenues in Dilworth from B. D. Heath.

Before the year was out a church had been built on the property, with help in the form of a "conditional donation" of $150 from the Board of Church Extension of the Methodist Episcopal Church, South, in Louisville, Kentucky. The property was conveyed to the new Dilworth Church 13 years later, when Mayer, Brem and Littlejohn are still listed as trustees of Trinity Church. The price in both transactions is given as $200.[17]

*The Atherton Church, ancestor of today's Dilworth United Methodist Church*

For two years the new Dilworth church would share a minister with another new church organized about the same time, Belmont Park.

The last new Methodist church established before the turn of the century was Belmont Park Methodist, begun in 1897 in what was then a developing neighborhood east of uptown known as Belmont Springs. The church had its start when the minister of Tryon Street Church, Dr. W. W. Bays, began holding meetings in the community.

Belmont Park erected a new sanctuary on Hawthorne Lane in 1953, but later dissolved itself to provide the nucleus of today's University City UMC.

In reviewing those historic old handwritten church deeds from so many years ago one is struck by a bit of language that appears repeatedly: "...the said premises shall be used, maintained, and disposed of as a place of divine worship for the ministry and membership of the Methodist Episcopal Church, South, subject to discipline, usages, and ministerial appointments, as from time to time authorized and declared by the General Conference of said church, and the annual conference within whose bounds the said premises are situated..." The language reflects a requirement established by John Wesley himself in the early days of the Methodist movement in England, known as the "trust clause." It was designed to ensure, among other things, that each local church would accept the ministers appointed to serve them. The clause, only slightly modified, is still in use today.[18]

## Chapter Notes

1. LeGette Blythe and Charles Brockmann, *Hornets' Nest, The Story of Charlotte and Mecklenburg County*, p. 167. The earlier log court house at the Square had been replaced in 1810 by a brick structure on the same site. The first courthouse away from the Square was erected in 1845 on the northeast corner of Trade and Church Streets.
2. James Jenkins, *Experience and Labours of James Jenkins*, p. 228.
3. Mildred Morse McEwen, *First United Methodist Church*, p. 19.
4. *Ibid.*, p. 18. The deed was recorded on April 2, 1834, and is found in Deed Book 23 at page 200, Mecklenburg County Register of Deeds Office.
5. The deed refers to lots 358 and 360. Each lot measured 6 poles by 12 poles (99 feet by 198 feet). Combined they were just under one acre.
6. McEwen, p. 25
7. Phillip E. Gerdes, *Historical Sketch of St. Mark's Evangelical Lutheran Church,* pp. 2-3.
8. According to the deed, the trustees of "Charlotte Colored Presbyterian Church" purchased the property from "F. W. Ahrens and wife Laura Ahrens," placing into question the tradition that it was purchased from the Lutheran congregation. However, Ahrens was a trustee of St. Mark's, and had also been involved in the original transaction when the Lutherans bought the property from the Methodists. Ahrens was active in buying and selling real estate. Between April 1867 and his death in 1914 he was named as "grantee" in 151 real estate transactions, almost all of them in what we now call "uptown." Generally, he and his wife, Laura, are both named on the deeds. From this, it appears most likely that Ahrens was acting as a broker for St. Marks, although he may have possessed the property briefly in his own name. The present First United Presbyterian Church building on that site was erected by the predecessors of the present congregation. It is not the original Methodist or Lutheran building.
9. The Capt. Brem mentioned in the article was undoubtedly Thomas H. Brem, son-in-law of David Dunlap. Brem commanded Company C, "Brem's Artillery," of the Tenth North Carolina Regiment.
10. *First Presbyterian Church,* an undated booklet prepared by the Finance and Stewardship Committee of the Board of Deacons of First Presbyterian Church. The accounts are puzzling. Photos of the Mecklenburg Courthouse in use during the Civil War, at the corner of Trade and Church streets, do not show a clock tower. The steeple of Tryon Street Methodist Church contained a bell, but no clock is visible. The Charlotte City Hall, at North Tryon and Fifth streets, did have a clock tower and bell which chimed the hour, but it was not built until 1891, well after the Civil War.
11. McEwen, p. 30.
12. This is the Zoar in southern Mecklenburg County. There was an even earlier Zoar in Iredell County, which was listed on the Sugar Creek Circuit as early as 1834.
13. McEwen., p. 50.
14. Most of this segment is based on an unpublished history provided by Memorial United Methodist Church.
15. McEwen, p. 42.
16. *Ibid.*, p. 50.
17. The Dilworth transactions are recorded in Book 110, page 571; Book 116, page 282; and Book 242, page 303; in the Mecklenburg County Register of Deeds office.
18. *Book of Discipline*, ¶2503.

# 11

# Into the Suburbs

At the dawn of a new century Charlotte was showing signs of the city it was to become. In 1908 J. A. Jones had erected one of the first skyscrapers in the Southeast, the 12-story Independence Trust Building. Among notable features of the bank was a separate door for women customers.

In 1911, George Stephens launched the Myers Park neighborhood on what had been his father-in-law's 1100-acre cotton plantation southeast of the city.

The Lance Plant opened in 1913, and by 1915 Ford Motor Company's Charlotte assembly line was rolling out two dozen new cars a day, with a sticker price of $400. Electric lights were a newly available convenience, with Southern Power Company, headed by "Buck" Duke, building hydroelectric plants on the Catawba River. Retail competition was going strong by 1900 when J. B. Ivey opened his Charlotte store.

News pages had stories of women seeking the right to vote. International headlines foreshadowed troubling times, with Europe increasingly threatened by war.

But the war hadn't come yet to Charlotte. On a sunny day, people with time to spare caught a trolley out to Lakewood Park on Tuckaseegee Road. Those fortunate (or brave enough) to own a car could go for a drive around town...if the roads weren't too dusty. Mayor Kirkpatrick employed water wagons to dampen the dust on Trade Street. For the less adventurous there was the Amuze-U movie theater.

Churches, too, were being built across Mecklenburg. As of 1900, the city of Charlotte had seven Methodist churches. More than a dozen others had been established in all parts of the county.

The first decade of the 20th century saw the creation of Huntersville, Spencer Memorial, Chadwick, Davidson, and Hunters Chapel. Duncan Memorial opened in 1911 on what was then the fringe of the city as Charlotte began to spread beyond its longtime boundaries.

The church later known as Central Avenue Methodist was started in 1913 in a brand new suburb on Central Avenue. Originally named First Methodist Protestant Church, it was part of a denomination created in 1830,[1] when Methodists split on the issue of lay participation in church leadership. It became Central Avenue Methodist in 1939, when the denominations reunited.

Thrift Methodist, northwest of the city, was organized in 1914.

By 1915 Charlotte's population numbered almost 40,000 people, and Methodists were in the forefront of the city's growth. More Charlotteans were moving to the suburbs and wanted churches closer to home. Tryon Street Church sought to meet this need by continuing its tradition of forming new congregations. Members of Tryon Street, led by department store owner J. B. Ivey, began the long process of organizing a church on Hawthorne Lane. It would join Dilworth as one of the city's great suburban churches, drawing charter members from Tryon Street, Trinity and Calvary churches.

*E. A. Cole...Along with J. B. Ivey and B. D. Heath, pictured elsewhere, he was among the founders of Hawthorne Lane United Methodist Church.*

In 1925 a church that would become one of Charlotte's largest was organized at the intersection of

Queens and Providence Roads. It was named Myers Park Methodist. Ironically, some of the founders of the still-young Hawthorne Lane Church would provide dynamic leadership in the new Myers Park congregation. Among them were B. D. Heath, Luther Snyder and Louis Asbury.[2]

In 1927 a milestone event occurred in Charlotte Methodism when Tryon Street and Trinity churches merged to form First Methodist. The story of "First Church" is told in more detail in the following chapter.

From 1920 to 1940, Charlotte's population more than doubled, and a survey found hundreds of residents who professed to be Methodists, but did not belong to a church. Hundreds more had no church affiliation at all, offering fertile ground for church extension. But after First Methodist opened its doors, church growth in Mecklenburg slowed. Homestead Methodist was organized in 1932. St. John's was formed as a non-denominational congregation in 1934, but did not become a Methodist church until 1942.

In that year, 1942, a group of farsighted Methodists, led by builder J. A. Jones, sensed the need to energize church growth, and decided to act. They formed the Charlotte City Mission Society, later renamed the District Mission Society. Jones was a member of Myers Park Methodist Church. His firm, J. A. Jones Construction Company, had built several churches, including Hawthorne Lane Methodist. Some of the others involved included Edwin L. Jones, Paul Ervin, A. W. Lawing, and Dr. Edgar Nease. District Superintendent Dr. Grover T. Bond was its first president.

At its founding the society set a goal of building one new Methodist church every year in the city of Charlotte "until Methodism reached the entire populace." Within a year Kilgo and St. John's were established.[3] Mouzon, St. James and Purcell came soon thereafter.[4] Within five years eight new Methodist churches were organized. St. Luke Methodist on Shamrock Drive, the society's tenth church, was organized in 1953. But it didn't stop there. Over 26 years, on average, one new church per year was started in the area now defined as the Charlotte District.[7] In addition to those already mentioned, a partial list of churches started or assisted by the District Mission Society includes Assurance, Central, Cokesbury, Commonwealth, Duncan Memorial, Good Shepherd, Grace, Morningstar, Providence, St. Stephen, Sharon, Tuckaseegee Road, and Wesley.

Probably no other single organization had more to do with the growth of Methodism in Mecklenburg County than the District Mission Society.

The impact of new church creation is demonstrated by the following figures: In 1951, the 42 churches of the Charlotte District reported a membership of 17,230 people. In 1968 these same 42 churches reported a membership of 21,487, an increase of about 19 percent. The 23 new churches formed in that period had 12,058 members, or 35 percent of the total district membership. In 1973 the 26 new churches established since 1941 reported a membership of 13,326. The Methodist membership in the Charlotte District had slightly more than doubled since 1941, but 80 percent of this gain was represented in those 26 new congregations.[8]

Women have often been the prime movers behind church growth in Mecklenburg County, and much of the church's most meaningful work has been spearheaded by women's groups.

The earliest Methodist women's organization in Mecklenburg was the Ladies Aid Society, formed by members of the old Tryon Street Church. Started as a sewing circle, they made aprons which they sold to raise money for the church budget. Among its members were Polly Dunlap, wife of Charlotte's Methodist founder, Dr. David Dunlap, and her sister, Mrs. Lillie Oates, wife of Brawley Oates.[8]

In 1878 the Women's Board of Foreign Missions was formed, joined eight years later by the Women's Board of Home Missions. This firmly established the focus on missions which is still a central feature of women's societies today. The Women's Missionary Society was organized in 1910.

In 1939, when Methodism's three main American branches were reunited, the women's groups were also reconstituted. Two groups emerged—the Women's Society of Christian Service (WSCS) and the Wesleyan Service Guild. The WSCS primarily attracted women who were not employed outside the home. Working women joined the Service Guild.

Yet another name change came after the 1968 merger of the Methodist Church and the Evangelical United Brethren, creating the United Methodist Church. The merger led, in 1973, to the establishment of The United Methodist Women.

Churches have always been at the forefront in promoting education. In the period before public schools became the norm, many private academies and "industrial schools" sprang up, some getting their start with help from neighborhood churches. One of the most prominent was Big Spring School, a forerunner of the later Berryhill School. The two-story school building was adjacent to the Big Spring Church, but apparently was not run by the church. Another was the Southern Industrial School, whose headmaster, the Rev. J. A. Baldwin, would later be called as pastor for the new Belmont Park Methodist Church.

An ambitious and enduring Methodist project in Charlotte is the institution now formally known as Aldersgate, but probably more familiar to most people as The Methodist Home.

Department store founder and active Methodist J. B. Ivey was among those who first proposed a Methodist retirement home in the area. He approached Eugene Cole, another leading Methodist, who had previously bought the Hezekiah Alexander farm, also known as the "Rock House Place" on Shamrock Drive. The farm consisted of 175 acres of land, plus the historic Alexander house, built in 1774. Ivey asked Cole about selling the property, but Cole offered to donate it. Cole's generosity was likely motivated by a longtime dream of his brother, the Rev. E. O. Cole, for providing a retirement home for ministers. A later gift from the Cole family enabled the home to buy

*Big Spring School, founded by members of Big Spring Methodist Church.*
*The photo was made about 1926*

an additional 50 acres, known as the Hagler Farm, enlarging the total site to 225 acres.

Plans for the retirement facility were presented to the 1944 Annual Conference, which was meeting, appropriately, at Myers Park Methodist Church. Bishop Clare Purcell was presiding. The facility was conceived as a home for "...retired ministers in the Western N. C. Conference; widows of retired ministers of the same area; teachers in church institutions within the territory of the conference; loyal servants of the churches belonging to the Western N. C. Conference; and members of other denominations who, through channels of church, personal service, and influence have made splendid contributions to the upbuilding of the spiritual kingdom." The planned size would accommodate 100 residents.[9]

The plan included provisions for individual cottages for retirees, along with recreational facilities and small plots where residents could have their own gardens. Early plans envisioned farm land on the property being cultivated to produce food for the residents.

The ground breaking was held on May 25, 1947. Sadly, Eugene Cole had died the previous year and did not get to see his brother's dream fulfilled.

Recognizing the historic value of the Alexander "rock house," officials of the Methodist Home leased it to the Daughters of the American Revolution for 99 years, at a fee of $1 per year. The lease has since been transferred to the Hezekiah Alexander Foundation, and the site is now occupied by the Charlotte Museum of History as well as the restored Alexander house.

In 1960 a lease was granted to the City of Charlotte for the site of Methodist Home Park. In 1973 about 20 acres was leased to the Western North Carolina Conference for the Conference Center. The building was completed in 1975.

Over the years the Methodist Home grew to include Epworth Place (the original campus and cottages), Asbury Care Center (an intermediate care facility), and the Wesley Nursing Center. In 1998, to reflect a more contemporary vision of its facility, the name was changed to "Aldersgate, A United Methodist Retirement Facility." In 2001 Aldersgate announced an ambitious expansion plan, including apartments, cottages and a community center. The Wesley Nursing Center was leased for a time to the operators of Charlotte's Presbyterian Hospital, but more recently was sold to a private company.

The 1950s saw a spurt of new churches organized in the county. Grace and St. Luke were followed by Providence, Aldersgate, and then, in quick succession, Cokesbury, St. Andrews, Blair Road, Christ, St. Mark's, Tuckaseegee Road and Plaza.

After that the pace slowed to about two churches per decade. Sharon was organized in 1966 and St. Stephen in 1968, both assisted by the District Mission Society. In 1972 there was Covenant (actually the product of a merger between Tuckaseegee Road and Wesley Heights), followed by Wesley in 1977. University City was formed out of Belmont Park in 1988, and St. Francis was organized in 1989. Good Shepherd (1991), Assurance (1996), and Light of Christ (1999) rounded out the millennium.

Two entirely new churches have come into being since the milestone year of 2000. They are Vermillion (2001), and Greater

Vision (2003). Morningstar also made its appearance, brought into being through efforts of the former Steeleberry United Methodist Church.

As the century drew to a close, Mecklenburg Methodists showed renewed energy in the field of assisting ethnic and immigrant groups in forming congregations and fellowships. The effort was spearheaded by a group called ReachOut, which initially was inspired by an outreach effort at Duncan Memorial UMC.

Beginning about 1981 Pastor Wade Rogers and the people of Duncan Memorial Church had been working with Cambodian children in Optimist Park. In 1988 the Charlotte District Council on Ministries began looking for ways to support and expand this ministry. One result of this work is the Cambodian Mission Church, a group which originally met at Spencer Memorial Church on 36th Street, and later moved to First Church uptown. They are led by a Cambodian minister, Sam Om.

Another group has actually become a church, named the First Hmong Church. They meet at Hickory Grove Methodist. The Rev. Cher Lue Vang is their pastor.

Other ethnic congregations formed in Charlotte are:

The Ghana Community Mission, led by Emmanuel K. B. Yiadom, worships at Big Spring UMC.

Agua De Vida Mission, a Hispanic congregation, meets at Memorial United Methodist Church. They are led by Augusto O. Caldera.

Victory UMC, a Native American congregation was formed and met for a time at St. Luke UMC, but has more recently moved to Union County.

## Chapter Notes

1. Some sources give the date as 1828. The date 1830 is the one used in the most recent (2000) edition of the *Discipline*.
2. G. W. Bumgarner says that Louis Asbury was a descendent of Daniel Asbury. This genealogy has not been traced.
3. St. John's had begun in 1934 as Oakhurst Mission, and later became the Oakhurst Interdenominational Church before affiliating with the Methodist Church in 1942.
4. Elmer T. Clark, *Methodism in Western North Carolina*, p. 146.
5. Mildred Gwin Andrews, *Myers Park United Methodist Church 50th Anniversary*, p. 81.
6. *Ibid.*
7. Mildred Morse McEwen, *First United Methodist Church*, p. 110.
8. Andrews, p. 16.

# 12

# First Church

Because of its prominence in Charlotte Methodism, its lineage from the city's original Methodist society, and its earlier status as the city's "cathedral church," First United Methodist deserves a separate chapter about its history.

Its name is commonly shortened to "First Church" and it is often called the "mother church" of Charlotte Methodism, but First Methodist did not officially come into being until October 28, 1927.[1]

To recap briefly, The original society in Charlotte, formed in 1818, built a church at Seventh and College about 1833; moved to Sixth and Tryon Streets in 1859 to become Tryon Street ME Church, South; then merged with its daughter church, "Charlotte Trinity," to become First Methodist.

At the time of the merger, both churches had grown to substantial size, even by today's standards. Tryon Street numbered nearly 1,400 members; Trinity had about 1,100.

The story of tobacco magnate James B. Duke's role in the merger has been retold countless times, and doubtless has been embellished over the years. As mentioned elsewhere, Duke was a Methodist and gave generously to Methodist causes. In one account, he desired an imposing, cathedral-style church for Charlotte, and encouraged the two major downtown churches to create it by merger. More credible versions suggest that the merger had been discussed among members of the two churches before they approached Duke. When it was first suggested, Duke reportedly demurred, saying he "didn't like churches that were too big for the people to know the preacher."[2]

But he obviously had further thoughts on the matter. When asked again, he is said to have offered $100,000 to go toward the cost.

In 1924 Duke created the Duke Endowment, naming a variety of church, educational and health care beneficiaries. First Methodist was not mentioned in the endowment, perhaps because the merger had not yet occurred, and more likely because his promise of funds was to be, for Duke, a relatively small onetime contribution. But he also neglected to formalize the pledge in any other record, even his will. Duke died on October 10, 1925.

It was more than a year after Duke's death that members of the two churches formally agreed to go through with the merger. The vote came at a combined quarterly meeting November 24, 1926.[3]

The new church was built of Indiana limestone on the site of the former Oates home, which fronted on Tryon Street. The property, stretching the full length of Eighth Street all the way back to Church Street, cost $140,000. Other adjoining property was purchased later. Few changes have been made in the appearance of the building since it was completed. The original chapel was converted into a multipurpose room in 1967, and renamed "Founders' Hall." Minor alterations were made on the north side in 1998 when the 19-story Odell Building was constructed next door.[4]

Members began using the building before the sanctuary was completed. The first service, October 30, 1927, was held in the adult Sunday School auditorium, now called Founders' Hall, with Bishop Edwin D. Mouzon leading the service. Lights had not yet been installed, so the first evening service was held in the nearby Carolina Theater. Bishop Mouzon again preached the first sermon in the new sanctuary on March 11, 1928. The first pastor was W. Walter Peele, who later became a bishop serving the Richmond, Virginia, area.

The two founding churches had counted on the sale of their existing buildings to provide significant funding for the new building. The Tryon Street property was sold for $250,000. However, buyers for the Trinity site did not come forward as hoped, and years elapsed before it was sold.[5] Compounding their problem was the financial crash of 1929. In hard times, members scrambled to repay the debts

*First Methodist Church, at the time of its dedication, March 1944.*

incurred in construction of the new building. Meanwhile, Doris, the only daughter of James B. Duke, had inherited much of her father's estate including the home called "Rough Point" in Newport, Rhode Island. In November 1933 she turned 21 years old. Shortly thereafter, at the church's request, an official of the Duke Endowment approached her regarding her father's promise, a decade earlier, to contribute to the merger.

At this point, several colorful variations of the story have been circulated. In one account, Miss Duke slipped into the church one Sunday morning and quietly dropped $100,000 into the offering plate. In another, the check arrived in the mail.

In the official version released by the church at the time, the source of the donation is not identified. As reported in *The Charlotte Observer* for March 5, 1934, "The First Methodist Church of this city has received from a friend whose name cannot be made public a gift of $100,000 to be applied on the church's building indebtedness."

The announcement to the congregation was made during the morning service of worship March 4 by Dr. W. Walter Peele, pastor of the church. Members immediately voted to launch a campaign to raise a matching amount to further reduce the debt. Still, it would take another ten years for the church to completely pay off its notes, an event which was celebrated with a dedication ceremony in March 1944.

Among notable gifts to the church over the years were the chimes in the tower, donated by Frank O. Sherrill in honor of his parents, the Rev. and Mrs. C. F. Sherrill. The chimes became a familiar sound in the center city, played every day at 12 noon and 5 p.m.

Members of First UMC have been at the forefront of Methodist benevolence to the community. As mentioned previously, in the mid 1940s Eugene M. Cole, Dr. L. B. Abernethy, Jackson Beall, W. Reynolds Cuthbertson, J. B. Ivey, George F. Ivey, Edwin L. Jones, H. L. McDougle, Frank O. Sherrill, and J. Luther Snyder were instrumental in founding the Methodist Home for the Aged on Shamrock Drive. Land for the home was given by Eugene Cole.[6]

Later, the Hagoods, Cuthbertsons and Van Hoys were among First Church members who led in planning and building the Wesley Nursing Center in the early 1960s.[7]

For some years the bishop of the Charlotte area maintained an office at First Church, resulting in its recognition as the "cathedral church." Annual Conferences were held there in 1938 and 1942.[7] In time Bishop Earl G. Hunt moved to the Cole Building on Hawthorne Lane, and, in 1976, to the Methodist Conference Center adjoining the Methodist Home on Shamrock Drive.

Having shed its mantle as the Methodist "cathedral," First Church today has turned its focus more sharply to serving the needs of its urban community. The church maintains a strong core of longtime members while welcoming newcomers from varied backgrounds, so that today it prides itself on being one of the most diverse congregations in the district.

## Chapter Notes

1.  Mildred Morse McEwen, *First United Methodist Church,* p. 59. The bulk of this chapter is based on Dr. McEwen's book. For brevity, only references of particular interest will be noted here.
2.  The statement by Duke is from an interview with a Duke associate, E. R. Bucher, a member of Trinity and First Methodist churches, recorded in 1963, and quoted by Dr. McEwen on p. 57.
3.  McEwen, p. 58
4.  The Odell complex includes an underground parking garage, also used by church members, which has two small above-ground access structures. The Structures were built of the same Indiana limestone as the original church building and closely match it in design.
5.  The site was sold in the late 1930s to the Federal Reserve Board for $100,000. A branch of the Federal Reserve Bank was built on the site, and it, in turn was later replaced by the existing building, Three Wachovia Center.
6.  LeGette Blythe and Charles Brockmann, *Hornets' Nest,* p. 334.
7.  McEwen, p. 175.

# 13

# Conference and District

Christian terminology must be confusing to outsiders. We even confuse ourselves at times.

For example, take the word "church." It may refer to the worldwide body of people who follow Jesus Christ. It may mean a denomination, such as the United Methodist Church. It may be a brick building with a steeple on top. Or it may be just a congregation of devout people who meet for worship in a rented auditorium.

Likewise, the word "conference" can have different meanings, and while the difference may seem trivial, it complicates research into the start of the Methodist conference as we know it today.

In today's United Methodist Church, the annual conference is an ongoing organization, with offices, a staff, boards and committees. In most cases, a conference has its own bishop. Because of this, when early writers referred to a "Virginia Conference" or a "South Carolina Conference," we tend to think there was a standing organization with day-to-day administrative functions. But in fact, those conferences were just meetings, held on a regional basis for the convenience of the widely scattered ministers. They had no offices, no paid staff, and no permanently appointed bishops. The presiding officers at the conferences were bishops who "itinerated" throughout the whole church.

In the beginning, all of American Methodism was a single administrative unit, with a single annual business meeting, called a conference. The first conference (meeting) of Methodist preachers in America was held in Philadelphia July 14, 1773.[1] Francis Asbury was present, but Thomas Rankin, who had arrived in the colonies only six weeks earlier, presided. Rankin had served as a traveling preacher for Wesley in England for 11 years, and as the senior Methodist in America, he was called "general assistant."[2] Probably no more than six or seven preachers attended the conference. In all, the movement numbered only ten preachers and six circuits—New York, New Jersey, Philadelphia, Baltimore, Norfolk and Petersburg. There were 1,160 members "in society."

Meetings were held annually thereafter, mostly in Baltimore, Philadelphia, and Virginia.

When the Revolution began, virtually all of the English preachers except Asbury returned home.[3] At that time, he became the unofficial leader of American Methodism. In 1779 a "preparatory" meeting was held in Delaware, before the regular conference in Fluvanna County, Virginia. During the Delaware meeting, the preachers in attendance determined that Francis Asbury should act as general assistant (chief administrator) of American Methodists.

Starting with the Delaware and Virginia meetings in 1779, each yearly conference involved separate meetings in different locations, mostly Baltimore and Virginia; sometimes Delaware, Philadelphia or North Carolina; but they all were counted as separate sessions of a single conference. By 1782, there were 26 circuits with 59 preachers, spread from North Carolina to New York. Because of the growth and spread of Methodism, it was decided to formalize the custom of holding two annual meetings. Since the "northern" conference (Baltimore) was older and better established, it was allowed greater policy-making authority. Any rules adopted at the "southern" conference (Virginia) did not apply if they conflicted with rules made in Baltimore. During these years preachers were being assigned to circuits in North Carolina at the meetings in Virginia.

In 1784 the regular annual meetings were again held in Virginia and Baltimore. Of far greater importance, however, was a third meeting that year which began on December 24 in Baltimore. This was the "Christmas Conference," at which American Methodists officially organized themselves as a church. The name, *Methodist Episcopal Church*, was suggested by John Dickins, whose first appointment in 1777 had been to the North Carolina Circuit.[4] From this time forward Methodist ministers could be ordained to administer the sacraments of baptism and communion.

Another General Conference would not be held until 1792. In 1789 a council of church leaders, including bishops Asbury and Coke, was established to provide oversight for the church between general conferences. However, the council proved to be unpopular and was abandoned after 1790. The 1792 meeting is now counted as the first General Conference.[5] They have been held every four years since.

North Carolina has earned a place in Methodist history as the site of the first annual conference after the church was organized. It was held on April 20, 1785, at the home of Green Hill in Louisburg, in what is now Franklin County.[6]

Jesse Lee counts the Louisburg meeting as the 14th Methodist conference in America. Beginning that year, the separate regional meetings were numbered individually, although the minutes continued to reflect the existence of only one administrative body.

Conferences were held annually in North Carolina every year from 1785 through 1794, including a second meeting at Green Hill's in Louisburg in January 1792 and another in December 1792.[7]

Methodism did not gain a foothold in South Carolina until Francis Asbury led an effort to establish a society in Charleston in 1785. Three circuits were recognized in South Carolina that year: Charleston, Georgetown and Broad River.

The first conference in South Carolina was held in 1787 in Charleston.[8] After this, conferences were held in South Carolina each year through 1803, the majority of them in Charleston, although one is simply recorded as "South Carolina" and three were held in Camden.

In 1804 the South Carolina Conference was held in Augusta, Georgia. Bishops Asbury and Coke presided. The conference had three districts that year–Saluda, Camden and a new one called Swanino. Both the Camden and Swanino districts had circuits extending into North Carolina, and Swanino had two circuits that were entirely in North Carolina.[9]

Historically, the bishop had set the time and place of the conferences. At the 1796 General Conference it was decided to limit the number of annual conferences to six, and the boundaries for each were set. These were to be New England, Philadelphia, Baltimore, Virginia, South Carolina and a "Western Conference." Four years later the number was expanded to seven, with New England being divided into New England and New York. At this time, the annual conferences still were not regarded as administrative entities, but merely as regional meetings.

The development of the "annual conference" as a year-round administrative body is ambiguous. Some writers point to 1802 as the formal beginning of the annual conference.[10] Lee uses the term "annual conference" for meetings as far back at 1792, but there is no evidence of an ongoing administrative function between meetings, other than that exercised directly by the bishops.

As the custom developed of holding regional conferences, the bishops would travel to preside at each conference, even in 1793 when there were as many as 19 separate conferences. Until 1800 there were only two bishops, and even when a third bishop (Richard Whatcoat) was elected, he was more of a replacement than an addition. Asbury was in declining health and Coke was spending a great deal of time in England. Not until 1824 did the church have more than three bishops at any one time.[11] When the Methodist Episcopal Church divided into separate northern and southern groups in 1844 there were still only five bishops.[12]

The North Carolina Conference was established in 1837, formed from districts which were previously in the Virginia Conference. Almost a third of the state, including Mecklenburg County, remained in the South Carolina Conference. In 1850, the North Carolina Conference picked up about a dozen southeastern counties from South Carolina, and, in 1870, assumed oversight of the remainder. Mecklenburg County, which had been part of the South Carolina Conference from the beginning, was now part of a North Carolina Conference.[13]

*Western North Carolina Conference Center, the United Methodist headquarters in Charlotte. The building is adjacent to Aldersgate, the United Methodist Retirement Community.*

Until 1890 the extreme western part of the state, including Asheville, had been part of the Holston Conference, based in Tennessee. In that year, the Western North Carolina Conference was born, taking over Holston's North Carolina districts, and a number of Piedmont counties which had been in the North Carolina Conference.[14] The boundary between the two North Carolina conferences was the eastern borders of Rockingham, Guilford, Randolph, Stanly and Anson counties.[15]

Although we commonly think of a bishop being appointed to an annual conference, the appointment is actually to an "episcopal area," and a bishop may preside over more than one annual conference. The bishop who presides at the Western North Carolina Annual Conference is officially the "bishop of the Charlotte Area," and serves as "president" of the annual meeting.

The concept of assigning bishops to episcopal areas began to take shape around 1900. Before this time, bishops were considered to itinerate within the church as a whole. The idea of regional assignments was adopted officially by the (northern) Methodist Episcopal Church at its General Conference in 1912. Previously, the 1882 General Conference of the MEC, South, recommended that bishops be spread throughout the conference, but took no official action to implement it. The 1939 union of Methodist bodies created the jurisdictional system and the practice of assigning bishops within the jurisdictional areas where they were elected.[16]

Bishops who lived in Charlotte before 1939 included John Kilgo, whose home was a prominent landmark on the Plaza at Belvedere. Bishop Edwin Mouzon was a Charlotte resident for many years, presiding at both the Western North Carolina and Upper South Carolina Conferences. He bought property in Dilworth in 1927 and lived there until his death in 1937.

Clare Purcell, who presided at Western North Carolina Annual Conferences from 1938 to 1948, was the first to have an official episcopal residence in Charlotte. He spent three years in an apartment on West 10th Street before moving into a home on Roswell Avenue. Within a short time he relocated to another house on the same street, which continued to serve succeeding bishops into the term of Earl G. Hunt. The current residence for Charlotte bishops was acquired by the conference during the tenure of Bishop Hunt.[17]

For some years the Charlotte area was within several overlapping conferences representing different branches of Methodism. In 1828 a disagreement over lay representation led about 5,000 members to separate from the Methodist Episcopal Church and form the Methodist Protestant Church. During its existence, this denomination had at least three churches in Mecklenburg County—First Methodist Protestant (which later became Central UMC), Zoar (now Zoar UMC), and Bethel Methodist Protestant Church.[18]

In 1844 another division, this time over the issue of slavery, resulted in creation of separate northern and southern bodies of the Methodist Episcopal Church. Almost all churches of the Charlotte area were part of the Methodist Episcopal Church, South. However, when the present-day Asbury UMC was organized as Asbury Chapel in 1865, it was a part of the (northern) Methodist Episcopal Church. The church which is now Oak Grove UMC, and Simpson Chapel, a forerunner of today's Simpson-Gillespie UMC, were also Methodist Episcopal Churches. Several other churches describe themselves as having been "Methodist Episcopal," but may have just inadvertently dropped the word "South" from their names.

The Methodist Protestant, Methodist Episcopal and Methodist Episcopal Church, South, reunited in 1939 to form the Methodist Church, and conferences of the respective groups were soon consolidated. The 1939 union created the jurisdictional system, placing African-American Methodists into the Central Jurisdiction. The Central Jurisdiction was dismantled in the 1968 merger of the Methodists with the Evangelical United Brethren, creating the United Methodist Church. Since 1968 all United Methodist churches in North Carolina and eight other states have been part of the Southeastern Jurisdiction.

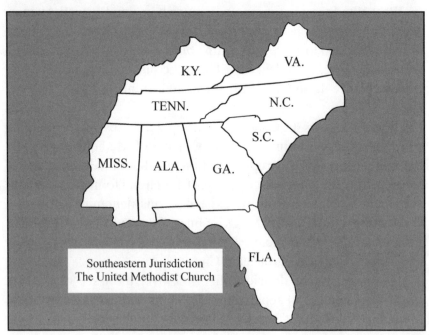

Southeastern Jurisdiction
The United Methodist Church

Prior to 1957 the Western North Carolina Annual Conference met in the fall of each year, rotating among most of the major cities and towns within the conference area. The conference was held in Charlotte 12 times, the most recent being September 1955, at Dilworth Church. Beginning in 1957 the meeting has been held at Lake Junaluska each June.

For some years, conference offices were divided between Charlotte and Statesville, although the bishop resided in Charlotte. The bishop's office was at the First Methodist Church. Later it was moved to the Cole Building on Hawthorne Lane, and in 1976 to the newly completed Conference Center on Shamrock Drive. When the Conference Center was built, all conference offices were consolidated in Charlotte.

# Circuits and Districts

In the early years Methodism was spread by "circuit riding" preachers who traveled continuously on horseback, depending on the charity of dwellers in lonely frontier cabins for food and a place to sleep.

The life of a circuit rider was hard, with little in the way of rewards other than the satisfaction of knowing that souls had been saved. In his *Pioneers of Methodism*, M. H. Moore relates a story about Francis Poythress, whose first appointment was the brand-new Carolina Circuit. Born into a well-to-do Virginia family, Poythress gave up a life of ease to follow his spiritual calling. Perhaps his only surrender to creature comfort was a tin of tea leaves, carefully packed in his saddle bag for the occasional evening when he might impose on his host to brew him a cup. On one particular night he handed the tin to the wife where he was staying, asking if she might prepare it for him. No doubt the lady had much experience cooking greens and fatback, but clearly tea was not in her repertoire. Emptying the can's contents into a pot, she boiled it vigorously, strained it, and placed the tea leaves on a plate. Presenting the plate to the preacher, she apologized that she had not been able to boil them down any further. "Madam," exclaimed the astonished reverend, "you have ruined my tea. It was the broth that I wanted."[19]

The original "circuit" is analogous to what we know today as a "charge," which is the assigned work of an individual pastor, or perhaps a senior pastor with one or more associate pastors. A circuit could consist of a dozen or more preaching places, spread over several counties. It might be laid out as a "three-week circuit" (or some other number), indicating how often the circuit rider would get to each preaching point. Worship was often held on days other than Sundays, and preaching outdoors was not uncommon, after a practice that Wesley and other Methodists had followed in England.

When groups of worshippers were organized, they were called "societies" or "classes," a style John Wesley had adopted earlier in England. Although the terms are sometimes used interchangeably, a class would normally have been a smaller group of ten to twelve people, sometimes part of a larger society. Each class would have a "class leader" who was responsible for the spiritual well being of the group.

Occasionally a society would have a "local preacher" and an "exhorter," lay persons who led services in the absence of the traveling, or itinerant preacher. A preacher who left the traveling ranks and settled down, as many did after they were married, was said to be "located." Occasionally a preacher would "locate" for a few years and then return to the traveling ministry.

A group of circuits was supervised by a minister called a "presiding elder." This was the beginning of districts as we know them today. (The term presiding elder was used into the 20th century, when it became "district superintendent.") The term "district" appears for the first time in conference records in 1801 .

Quarterly meetings of the circuit, similar to present-day charge conferences, would be attended by class leaders, lay preachers, exhorters and stewards from societies within the circuit, as well as the circuit preacher and, if there was one, a "junior preacher." Meetings were led by the presiding elder.

Business conducted at the quarterly meetings included examining and licensing prospective local preachers and exhorters, hearing appeals of persons expelled from societies for such offenses as "intemperance," and receiving monies collected by the societies for the support of the itinerant preachers.

The earliest Methodist preachers in North Carolina came down from circuits in southern Virginia, particularly in the eastern part of the state. The Brunswick Circuit, apparently centering on the area of present-day Brunswick County, Virginia, was especially prominent in early Methodist histories. There are references to a Mecklenburg Circuit, but it was also in Virginia, not Mecklenburg County, North Carolina.

The Carolina Circuit was established at the conference in Baltimore on May 21, 1776. It would be replaced two years later by the Tar River, Roanoke and New Hope Circuits.

In 1780 the Yadkin Circuit was established, including Mecklenburg, Lincoln, Rutherford, Burke, and Rowan Counties and "Yadkin Valley." It extended to Asheville and beyond. Andrew Yeargin was the preacher. Technically, all of Mecklenburg County was in the Yadkin Circuit, although we have no record of regular preaching in Mecklenburg at that time.

Some would say Bethel Church at Midland was Mecklenburg's first organized Methodist society, having been started about 1782. Cabarrus County, including Midland, was a part of Mecklenburg until 1792.

However, in present-day Mecklenburg, Harrison Church below Pineville is regarded as first. Harrison's (as it was known then) was formed about 1785, and was in the Santee Circuit when it was set up in 1787. By 1790, Harrison's was listed in the Catawba Circuit, also operating mainly in South Carolina.[20] That circuit clearly took its name from the Catawba River, not the county of that name in North Carolina.

Daniel Asbury organized the Lincoln Circuit in 1790, taking in parts of Mecklenburg County. Jesse Richardson was later appointed to assist in that circuit. The following year Asbury organized the Rehobeth Methodist Church at Terrell, in what is now Catawba County, the first Methodist church west of the Catawba River.

In December 1814 the Sugar Creek Circuit was established, as part of the Catawba District of South Carolina. This was the last South Carolina Conference attended by Bishop Francis Asbury. Churches or "preaching places" listed in the Sugar Creek Circuit that year included Charlotte, Harrison's, Martin's (now Trinity), and Christenbury's (a forerunner of today's Asbury UMC). There were additional preaching places in Anson, Cabarrus, Iredell and Rowan Counties. (Union County was not set apart from Mecklenburg until 1842.) William Barnett was the circuit preacher. Samuel Harrison had previously "located" (quit the itinerant ministry), but was still actively preaching. At the May 1815 quarterly conference of the Sugar Creek Circuit, one order of business was a recommendation that Harrison be readmitted as a traveling preacher. Harrison and Barnett were involved in organizing the first society at Martin's, which later became Buckhill and Trinity.

Until 1825 the Sugar Creek Circuit remained in the Catawba District. In that year it became part of the Cheraw District, and in 1828 shifted to the Lincolnton District.

In 1834 Sugar Creek Circuit became the Charlotte Circuit. At times, the circuit included as many as 60 or 70 "preaching places." In 1868 a separate South Charlotte Circuit was spun off with eight churches. The remaining circuit continued to be called just "Charlotte," or in some sources, "North Charlotte."

The Charlotte District was formed in 1853, including the Charlotte Circuit and circuits in Union and Anson counties.[21]

In 1863 we again see a Catawba District, and five years later a Shelby District encompassing circuits in Mecklenburg County. The Charlotte District was reestablished in 1872.

The Charlotte District was part of the original group constituting the Western North Carolina Conference when it was formed in 1890. By 1900, when the conference had eleven districts with a total membership of just over 72,000, the Charlotte District reported 8,055 members.[22]

## Chapter Notes

1. Much of this chapter is based on Jesse Lee's *A Short History of the Methodists in the United States of America*, published in 1810, which provides a year-by-year summary of all annual Methodist conferences between 1773 and 1809. To avoid excessive notes, only references to other sources will be listed hereafter.
2. He was an "assistant" to John Wesley, who was the head of the Methodist movement.
3. Albert Deems Betts, *History of South Carolina Methodism*, p. 41.
4. *Ibid.*, p. 44. Also see M. H. Moore, *Pioneers of Methodism*, p. 108.
5. *Discipline* (2000 edition), p. 11.
6. Sarah I. Davis, *Covenant Made on Earth*, pp. 16-17.
7. *Ibid.*, pp. 18-19. The December 1792 meeting was counted as part of the 1793 conference. There is a minor variation of dates among different sources. Davis uses dates from *Asbury's Journal*. It is interesting that historical writers do not refer to the existence, during this period, of a "North Carolina Conference."
8. Jesse Lee does not include this conference in his account for 1787. However, Asbury relates in his journal that both he and Dr. Coke were in Charleston for a conference March 25-29, 1787. It is also mentioned by Betts in his *History of South Carolina Methodism* (p. 60), although he gives it the date of March 22. Perhaps the reason Lee did not mention it is that, according to Betts, no minutes of the meeting have been preserved.
9. Betts, p. 109.
10. Elmer T. Clark, *Methodism in Western North Carolina*, p. 24.
11. Determined from list of bishop elections in the *Discipline*.
12. *Discipline,* p. 14.
13. Clark, p. 67.
14. *Ibid.*
15. *Ibid.*, p. 168
16. Information provided by the Methodist Library at Drew University. During the time it existed as a separate denomination, the Methodist Protestant Church did not have bishops.
17. Information extracted from Charlotte City Directories.
18. This Bethel Methodist (different from the older Bethel in Cabarrus County) no longer exists, but its congregation was involved in forming Oak Grove Methodist Episcopal Church. According to tradition, a new building was being erected for the Bethel church, but it was never finished and the wood was used in constructing Oak Grove.
19. Moore, p. 87. This event may have occurred some time after Poythress moved on from his service in North Carolina. Moore attributes the story to a publication named *Early Times in Middle Tennessee*.
20. This is based on information in various histories of Harrison Church. The South Carolina Conference office in Spartanburg could not supply records of circuits prior to 1813.
21. Clark, p. 34.
22. *Ibid.*, p. 38.

# 14

## Some Notable Names

Through the years countless individuals have played significant roles in the growth and development of Methodism in Mecklenburg County. It would be impossible to identify them all, but some names appear repeatedly in historical documents and will be mentioned here.

David Dunlap was among the charter members of Tryon Street Church when it was organized in 1859, just two years before his death in 1861. A full chapter is devoted to his uniquely colorful story. Dunlap's daughter, Harriet, and son-in-law, Thomas Brem, were also among Tryon Street's charter members.

Born in 1816, Col. Thomas H. Brem was married first, probably about 1842, to Martha Fox, a descendant of the prominent Erwin family of Burke County. They had five children. Stephen Fox Brem, born in 1844, died as an infant two years later. Charles Francis Brem, born in 1846, grew up to be a physician and died in 1910 at age 64. Walter Brem, born July 31, 1849, died in 1925. Thomas H. Brem, Jr., was born in 1853 and died at age 29 in 1882. Mattie A. Brem was born in 1854 and died in 1857.[1] When Martha Fox Brem died in 1857, Col. Brem then married Harriet Dunlap Jones, daughter of David R. Dunlap and Mary "Polly" Lowrie. Brem was about 42 years old at the time. Harriet would have been about 37. She had also been married previously, to Dr. Edmund A. Jones of Caldwell County. Limited research did not reveal any children born to the marriage of Col. Brem and Harriet Dunlap Jones.

T. H. Brem was a director of Charlotte's first locally-owned bank, the Bank of Charlotte.[2] He is the Captain Brem mentioned in a newspaper account of Charlotte church bells being cast into weapons for the Civil War.[3] Brem commanded Company C ("Brem's Artillery") of the Tenth North Carolina Regiment. It would have been after this date that he acquired the rank of colonel, by which he was known following the war.

The Brem family was destined to play a prominent role in banking, insurance and real estate development in Charlotte during the early years of the 20th century.

Col. Brem's son Walter is the most interesting in terms of Charlotte history. He was co-owner, with William H. Martin, of a hardware store on the southeast corner of Trade and Tryon Streets, the spot marked today by Arnaldo Pomodoro's bronze "Grande Disco" sculpture at the Bank of America Plaza. Later he headed Walter Brem and Sons, general agents for Travelers Life Insurance Company for western North Carolina.[4]

He married Hannie Caldwell, a daughter of Governor Todd Robinson Caldwell of Morganton. They had four children, Walter Jr., who became a physician; Todd R., Mina (Mrs. Robert A. Mayer), and Helen ( Mrs. R. R. Beatty). The Walter Brems and two of their children, Walter Jr. and Mina, are listed among members of Tryon Street Church who transferred to Trinity when that church was formed in 1896.[5]

Walter Brem was one of three trustees representing Trinity Church in the sale of property at Cleveland and Worthington Avenues in Dilworth to the Dilworth M.E. Church in 1909. The lot had been purchased in 1896 from B. D. Heath.[6] Heath, like Brem an active Methodist, was a prominent businessman, developer and president of Charlotte National Bank, and would later donate the land for Hawthorne Lane Methodist Church.

The names of Brem, B. D. Heath, F. C. Abbott and George Stephens are intertwined in the history of Charlotte residential development. Abbott was treasurer and general manager of Piedmont Realty, formed by Brem and Heath. Stephens, vice president of the realty company, was a college roommate and fraternity brother with Walter Brem, Jr., at the University of North Carolina. He would later develop the Myers Park neighborhood on land owned by his father-in-law, John Springs Myers. Piedmont Realty developed Piedmont Park near Seventh Street and Central Avenue.[7] Heath was involved in developing the Elizabeth neighborhood

Walter Brem had an active role in the Charlotte public school system and the YMCA. He died February 11, 1925 and is buried near other members of the Brem family in Elmwood Cemetery. The Walter Brem residence at 211 East Boulevard in Dilworth remains today and has been designated a local historic site.

Another name associated with Dr. Dunlap is that of Brawley Oates. According to Alexander, Oates was a native of Cleveland County and probably came to Mecklenburg about 1830 or 1832. He married Lilly Lowrie, a sister of David Dunlap's wife, Polly Lowrie. Together the two men served numerous roles in church and civic life of their day. Oates was a town commissioner in 1833, and served as clerk of the county court from 1836 to 1842, and again from 1845 to 1854.[8]

He is first mentioned in minutes of the Charlotte Circuit on June 4,1836, when he was elected a steward of the circuit, and he appears regularly thereafter. In 1838 he was a trustee of the Big Spring Camp Ground (forerunner of Big Spring Church), an office to which he was reappointed several times.

As noted elsewhere, sisters Lilly Oates and Polly Dunlap were active in the formative years of the Ladies' Aid Society, forerunner of United Methodist Women.

Because of ill health in his later years, Oates moved to Florida, where he recovered and lived another 18 years.

In those same early years, two men known by their initials "J. B." came to Charlotte. Each was destined to play a pivotal role in the story of Methodism. By coincidence, both were the sons of men named Washington, and both began life in families of modest means. One was the son of a Methodist minister; the other, the son of a tobacco farmer. They were Joseph Benjamin Ivey and James Buchanan Duke.

*Joseph Benjamin Ivey*                    *James Buchanan Duke*

Probably no Methodist layman has been more active as a leader in multiple churches than J. B. Ivey. At various times he was a prime mover in Charlotte Trinity, Tryon Street and First Methodist churches, as well as a principle founder of Hawthorne Lane Methodist Church. In addition to his work in local churches, Ivey served the Western North Carolina Conference as chairman of the Board of Hospitals and Homes, and chairman of the Committee on Bible Teaching in the North Carolina Public Schools.[9]

Ivey was born on June 8, 1864 in Shelby, N. C., the son of devout Methodist parents, the Rev. George Washington Ivey and Selina Neal Ivey. He was the fifth of eight children, seven of whom survived to adulthood. Church work would always be a central part of his life. At the age of 14 he became a Sunday School teacher at a church in Denver, N.C. At 21 he was elected Sunday School superintendent of Kadesh Methodist Church in Belwood, in Cleveland County.

As a result of childhood measles Ivey suffered from poor eyesight, and his family felt that he would have difficulty in college.

So it was decided that he would learn a trade. At the age of 16 he was apprenticed to a cabinetmaker, for $40 a year plus room and board. Soon, however, he found his way into a more agreeable occupation which would turn out to be his life's work: retail merchandising.

Joseph Ivey's first job experience was in a small store in Belwood. Later he was a department manager for dry goods and hardware at the Henrietta Mills company store in Henrietta, in Rutherford County, moving on to manage a store in nearby Caroleen. He enjoyed the work, but believed he could do better, and nurtured an ambition to own his own business. Meanwhile, he had fallen in love with a young woman named Emma Gantt. They were married on February 2, 1893, and finances were tight. He began to explore options. He first looked at Greensboro, but decided "there was a better opening in Charlotte."

For about $25 a month, he rented space for a small store a block and a half from the Square on North Tryon Street, opening on February 18, 1900. First day sales amounted to $33.18. For deliveries he employed a boy on a bicycle.

Ivey believed his store was too far from the center of business activity. "This was farther out than any of the other dry goods stores," he would write, "but everybody said that Charlotte was getting to be so much of a city that all couldn't have a place around the square." He added, "After 40 years, that particular stand is still too far out for a dry goods store." Within a year he bought out a competitor in the first block of West Trade, moving into the new location between Christmas and New Year's Day.

By 1924, Ivey's had moved to an imposing five-story building on North Tryon Street. After being enlarged in 1934 the Ivey's building stretched the entire block along Fifth to Church Street. Together with Efird's and Belk, they would dominate retail merchandising in downtown Charlotte for much of the 20th century.

Soon after arriving in Charlotte Ivey joined Trinity Methodist Church on South Tryon Street. His flair for creative activities to boost church involvement quickly revealed itself. One of his ideas was to take youth on outings via the trolley to his home on South Boulevard.

But he could not stay long in one place. The following year he moved to a home on North Poplar Street, and transferred his membership to the Tryon Street Methodist Church. A year later he had moved again, and once more became a member at Trinity. About 1904 he returned to Tryon Street Church. Ivey writes fondly of his experience teaching and leading the Sunday School programs at both churches. At one point, he even learned to be an amateur magician to entertain boys in his Sunday School class.

By 1915 Ivey had bought a home on Central Avenue, near Charlotte's new suburb of Elizabeth. He joined efforts to launch a new church in that area, and became a founding member of Hawthorne Lane Methodist Church. He was so active in forming the new congregation that James B. Duke jokingly referred to it as "Ivey's church."

At Hawthorne Lane he again assumed the familiar office of Sunday School superintendent, and furnished a continuing stream of ideas to invigorate the new church. One of his ideas was to begin a "family night" to boost attendance at evening prayer meetings. A kitchen and dining room were set up in the basement where, for 35¢, a meal could be had, followed by an interesting program and a short sermon in the sanctuary. His gifts to the church included a set of chimes for the bell tower.

About 1925 Tryon Street and Trinity churches uptown decided to merge, forming First Methodist, and shortly thereafter Ivey transferred his membership again, to the new church. In his memoirs he notes, "It has always been my policy to change my church work every four or five years," a practice he acquired from his father, whose pastoral appointments forced the family to pull up its roots every few years. His reference was specifically to changing the duties he held in his church, but it could have applied as well to his changing of churches. He spent his remaining years as a member of First Methodist.

Ivey was a devout Methodist who took his religion seriously. For years the downtown store drew drapes over its windows on Sundays, lest passersby would be tempted to window shop. For many years the store would not sell such items as wine glasses or liquor decanters. He was an active lay leader in each of his churches, serving on administrative boards, forming youth groups, teaching Sunday School, and organizing at least one Epworth League (forerunner of the United Methodist Youth Fellowship).

Ivey died April 4, 1958, at the age of 94, and is buried in Elmwood Cemetery. The Ivey's chain was sold to the Marshall Field company in 1980, but retained its name until it was sold again, to the Dillards chain, in 1990.

James Buchanan "Buck" Duke was born in 1856, son of a Durham tobacco farmer, Washington Duke. He had one older brother, Benjamin.[10]

After the Civil War, Washington Duke and his two sons launched a tobacco manufacturing business, "W. Duke and Sons Co." In 1884 they began mass producing cigarettes, which would eventually become their main product. Young Buck Duke went to New York to peddle the products of the family firm. In 1890 he formed American Tobacco Company. At its height, in 1911, American Tobacco controlled 92 percent of the world's tobacco business. The company thrived until it was broken up under the Sherman Antitrust Act in 1911.[11]

In the meantime, Buck Duke and his brother Ben had become interested in hydroelectric power generation, and by 1898, had begun buying land along the Catawba River in North and South Carolina. At the same time, two other brothers, Doctors Walker Gill Wylie and Robert H. Wylie, had also become interested in the potential of harnessing water power to generate electricity and persuaded the Dukes to invest in the venture.

In 1905 Buck Duke and the Wylie brothers incorporated the Southern Power Company. Shortly before Duke's death in 1925 the company was renamed "Duke Power Company."

As a staunch Methodist, Duke provided handsomely for church-related causes.

In 1922 when Dilworth Methodist began planning for its new building on East Boulevard, Duke pledged $50,000 for the construction, a pledge on which he made good. As related elsewhere,

Duke also had a hand in the creation of Charlotte's First United Methodist Church, through the merger of two older churches, Tryon Street and Trinity Methodist.

In 1924, a year before his death, he established the Duke Endowment, signing the papers in the east wing of the Duke mansion in Charlotte. The endowment provides continuing income for Duke University, Furman University, and two schools in Mecklenburg County–Davidson College and Johnson C. Smith University. It also contributes to not-for-profit health care institutions in North and South Carolina, not-for-profit residential children's programs and adoption services, rural United Methodist churches and retired ministers in North Carolina.

Over the years the Methodist-related Duke University in Durham has been especially blessed with gifts from the Duke family. However, contrary to popular belief, the school was not named for "Buck" Duke. According to the university, it was named for his father, Washington Duke, who had also been a major benefactor.[12]

James B. Duke died October 10, 1925 at the age of 69. Doris, his only daughter, died in October 1993. She was 80 years old.

B. D. Heath, Charlotte businessman, banker, and developer, was a leader in the old Tryon Street Methodist Church and was among the founders of two of the city's most prominent United Methodist churches–Hawthorne Lane and Myers Park. He was president of Charlotte National Bank (chartered in 1897 and later merged into Wachovia).[13] With Walter Brem, Sr. and F. C. Abbott, he formed the Piedmont Realty Company, which developed Piedmont Park, around Seventh Street and Central Avenue. Heath then acquired additional property around Central and Hawthorne, which became the Oakhurst community.[14] His land holdings included the property he donated to Hawthorne Lane Methodist Church when it was organized in 1915. He was among a group that established the Charlotte Speedway near Pineville in the 1920s.[15] Mrs. Heath was one of the leaders in founding the Charlotte YWCA.[16]

Few names have become more closely associated with Methodism in Charlotte than that of the Cole family. Repeatedly, in searching Methodist records one encounters the brothers Eugene M. Cole, Eusebius A. Cole, and the Rev. Edwin O. Cole. The Coles were born in Chatham County not far from Chapel Hill, and grew up on the family farm near Carthage in Moore County.

Eugene Cole invented and patented a seed planting implement that would become the first product of a company he and his brothers established in 1900.[17] Their first operations were housed in a wooden building near the railroad crossing on Central Avenue. In 1911 they completed the complex of brick buildings which became an industrial landmark on Hawthorne Lane, near Central.

Cole Manufacturing Company prospered, and by 1980 was described in a *Charlotte News* article as one of the world's largest manufacturers of seed planting and fertilizing equipment.[18]

E. M. Cole was known for his generous financial support for Methodist institutions. He established the Eugene M. Cole Foundation in 1940 to provide funds for superannuated (retired) Methodist ministers and their widows. The initial endowment was $700,000.[19] He established scholarships for ministerial students at Duke University and Brevard College.[20]

In October 1943 he donated 175 acres of land which became the core property for the Methodist Home for the Aged on Shamrock Drive, helping fulfill a dream of his brother, the Rev. E. O. Cole.

The Cole Building, an office structure on Hawthorne Lane across from Presbyterian Hospital, became the seat of the Western North Carolina Conference when Bishop Earl. G. Hunt established offices there. The offices were moved in 1976 to the new Methodist Center, adjacent to the Methodist Home on Shamrock Drive.[21]

Eugene's younger brother E. A. Cole, along with J. B. Ivey, B. D. Heath, and others, was instrumental in organizing Hawthorne Lane Methodist Church in 1915. At the time of his death, *The Charlotte Observer* commented, "He was widely known as one of the leading

Methodist laymen to be found anywhere." He was among the leaders in developing the Methodist assembly grounds at Lake Junaluska, and served a number of years as chairman of the board of commissioners there. He was repeatedly elected a delegate to annual and general conferences of the Methodist Church.[22] E. A. Cole's daughter, Jean Cole Hatcher, served as president of Cole Manufacturing from 1953 to her retirement in 1972.

While his brothers excelled in the business world, E. O. Cole turned his talents to spiritual pursuits, becoming a Methodist minister in the Western North Carolina Conference. His appointments included the Derita Methodist Church, which he came to serve in 1938. The church was later renamed Cole Memorial in his honor. As mentioned previously, it was largely through his efforts that the Methodist Home for the Aged was established with a substantial gift from his brother.

J. A. Jones and his sons have been stalwarts of Methodism in Charlotte for more than a century. As a teenager, James Addison "Jim" Jones worked as a laborer, helping build Charlotte's first cotton mill. In 1890 he started his first contracting business, which, over the years, erected some of Charlotte's most prominent buildings. These included the Independence Building at the Square, store buildings for Belk, Ivey, and Efird, Hotel Charlotte, Carolina Theater, and the old Charlotte Observer Building.[23]

Some of the best work was on Charlotte churches. They built the Hawthorne Lane sanctuary in 1916 and, in 1940, the educational building for Dilworth Methodist.

The company was incorporated in 1920, with Jim and two of his sons, Raymond and Edwin, as the sole stockholders. Their numerous government projects included an air base in the Panama Canal Zone, an entire shipyard, and part of the government's top secret nuclear facility at Oak Ridge, Tennessee.[24]

J. A. Jones and his family were members of Tryon Street church before the formation of Trinity, but transferred to the new church when it was opened in 1896. A member of the church later recalled that the Jones family took up an entire pew in the church.[25] In 1926, when Trinity voted to rejoin Tryon, forming First Methodist Church, Jones was strongly opposed, and moved his membership to Dilworth.

The Jones family became substantial contributors to the Dilworth Church in both time and money. It was Mr. Jones and his son, Edwin, who first proposed the new educational building which the Jones company then constructed. Later it would be named in honor of J. A. Jones.

J. A. Jones was also one of the principal founders of the Charlotte District Mission Society in 1942, which was largely responsible for the dramatic growth of Methodism in Mecklenburg County from that period and many years thereafter.[27]

In later years Raymond A. Jones became a faithful member of Myers Park Methodist Church. His gifts to the church included funds to buy a neighboring residence which came to be known as the "Kindergarten House."[26] Over the years, the Jones family has been generous to Methodist causes, including hundreds of thousands of dollars contributed for new church construction. Edwin L. Jones, Sr., served as treasurer of the World Council of Methodism.[28]

This chapter could be extended indefinitely, honoring scores of others who have contributed to Methodism in Mecklenburg over the years. Surely there are many who deserve recognition, for they have laid the foundation for the active and thriving United Methodist Church we have today. To paraphrase William Henry Foote, the present is a reflected image of the past. It is only by knowing and understanding the world of our ancestors that we can fully appreciate the world we have today.

## Chapter Notes

1. Information from grave markers and records of Elmwood Cemetery, Charlotte, N.C.
2. LeGette Blythe and Charles Brockmann, *Hornets' Nest*, p. 303.
3. Article, *Western Democrat* [newspaper], May 6, 1862, p. 3.
4. Kratt, Mary and Thomas Hanchett, *Legacy: The Myers Park Story,* p. 19.
5. Mildred McEwen, *First United Methodist Church*, p. 42.
6. Deeds recorded in Book 110, page 571, and Book 242, page 303, Mecklenburg County Register of Deeds Office.
7. Kratt, pp. 19-20.
8. J. B. Alexander, *History of Mecklenburg County*, p. 177.
9. Most of this information about Ivey, except where noted otherwise, is based on his autobiography, *My Memoirs* .
10. Much of the information about James B. Duke, except where noted otherwise, is from *Duke Power, The First 75 Years*, by Joe Maynor.
11. "About Good Health-A Long History of Tobacco," by Gene Borio, The Tobacco BBS, www. tobacco.org.
12. This paragraph is based on information in an article written by Duke University archivist William E. King.
13. Blythe and Brockmann, p. 305.
14. F. C. Abbott, *50 Years in Charlotte Real Estate*, pp. 9, 18. Heath's Oakhurst development was not the same as today's Oakhurst neighborhood along Monroe Road.
15. Blythe, p. 436.
16. *Ibid.*, p. 377
17. *Ibid.*, p. 275.
18. *The Charlotte News*, July 2, 1980, p. 2B.
19. Elmer T. Clark, *Methodism in Western North Carolina*, p. 118.
20. *The Charlotte Observer*, June 27, 1944, p. 1.
21. McEwen, p. 175.
22. *The Charlotte Observer*, February 10, 1943, p. 1.
23. Mary Kratt, *Charlotte, Spirit of the New South*, p. 196.
24. *Ibid.*, p. 197.
25. McEwen, p. 51.
26. Mildred Gwin Andrews, *Myers Park United Methodist Church,* 1975, p. 25.
27. *Ibid.*, p. 81
28. McEwen, p. 133.

# 15

# Today's Churches

This chapter profiles each of the existing United Methodist churches in Mecklenburg County, with emphasis on how they began. The dates and other details were provided by the individual churches, supplemented with information from conference files and other sources.

A diligent effort was made to obtain information from all United Methodist Churches in the county. Some provided more information than others. Obviously, the older churches have more history to relate than the newer ones. The relative length of the profiles should not reflect on the importance of the churches. They simply reflect the amount of information available to us at the time of publication.

## Aldersgate UMC

Aldersgate United Methodist Church on Nations Ford Road was founded October 6, 1957, with 56 charter members. The Charlotte District Mission Society helped the members buy land and erect their first building. Aldersgate shares its facilities with an African-American congregation, Wilson AME Church, and participates in the Room In The Inn program which provides winter shelter to Charlotte's homeless. A popular recurring event at Aldersgate is a churchwide "Fifth Sunday Luncheon," which is held in any month when there is a fifth Sunday.

*Aldersgate United Methodist Church*

# Asbury UMC

As mentioned in a previous chapter, it is not always easy to establish the date a church began. By any measure, Asbury United Methodist Church is one of the oldest in Mecklenburg County. D. A. Tomkins, in his *History of Mecklenburg County and the City of Charlotte*, says Bethesda, forerunner of Asbury Church, was established about 1810, by Andrew Moore. The noted historian Dr. J. B. Alexander, in his book, *Reminisces of the Past Sixty Years*, goes even further to say "Andrew Moore was the founder of Methodism in Mecklenburg County." The church's own history has a more modest account. It says in 1814 a Methodist fellowship was organized in the Ferrelltown area in northwestern Mecklenburg County. As with many other Methodist groups, these devout people had been stirred by a camp meeting, in this case a meeting held on the banks of the Black River. The society was known at first as "Christenburys," probably for Daniel Christenbury, the first class leader. The name became "Nazareth" and then "Bethesda" as the congregation moved their meeting places. If Asbury counts its origin from the formation of that first society, it would have been started about the same time as rural Trinity, which is generally regarded as the second-oldest Methodist Church in the county.

Andrew Moore had also established Moore's Camp Ground, which was especially popular as a meeting place for the Sugar Creek Circuit preachers and class leaders. Beginning in 1826, the circuit held its September meetings at Moore's Camp Ground almost every year for a number of years. Moore himself served as a class leader, exhorter and steward for many of those same years.

Asbury Chapel was formally organized in 1865. Their first building was constructed on two and one-half acres of land donated by Richard Jordan, about a quarter mile west of its present location. According to church tradition, it was named for Bishop Francis Asbury.

In 1900 work started on a new building. The framework had just been completed when a storm on March 6, 1901, destroyed the entire structure. Not deterred, members started working again, and by 1904 the new church was in use. The little white country church served its members for almost 60 years until being torn down to make room for a new structure. The new sanctuary was used for the first time in March 1963. In June 1987 the Fellowship Hall burned and was replaced by a new building in time for homecoming Sunday, August 20, 1989.

# Assurance UMC

Assurance United Methodist Church was formed in 1996 through the merger of Chadwick and St. James churches.

Chadwick, started in 1903, was located on Gossett Avenue in the Hoskins neighborhood.

St. James was established in 1943 with a membership of 51 persons. By the time the charter roll had been closed, membership had more than doubled, to 107. Their first meetings were held in a tent, provided by the District Mission Society. As winter weather brought colder temperatures, they moved indoors to the Thomasboro Industrial Arts Building. The Mission Society had acquired a lot for the new church at Thrift Road and Bradford Drive. Construction began in February 1946 and the building was ready for its first service on Christmas Sunday, December 25, 1946.

Both churches thrived in their early years, but as neighborhood patterns shifted, membership began to decline. In 1996 they decided to revitalize their programs by merging to form a new church in a new location. At first known as the Northwest Mecklenburg Mission, the congregation met for a time in the Christian Life Center at Paw Creek Presbyterian Church. The church now has a permanent home on Mount Holly-Huntersville Road and is looking forward to a bright future.

# Big Spring UMC

Big Spring United Methodist Church was officially organized on Sunday, October 14, 1866, although its true beginning was many years earlier. A centennial celebration of camp meetings at Big Spring was held in 1912, indicating the site had been used for religious gatherings even before the earliest Methodist records were kept in Mecklenburg County. If the church used this as its starting date, it would be among the three or four oldest churches in Mecklenburg County. The earliest tombstone in the church cemetery is for Elizabeth Walker, who died January 8, 1844.

Big Spring was first listed as a preaching place on the Charlotte Circuit in 1836. For a number of years the Charlotte Circuit, which covered most of Mecklenburg and parts of several surrounding counties, held quarterly conferences at the Big Spring Camp Ground. Stewardship records list Big Spring as one of the strongest societies in the circuit.

In 1834, 26 acres in Berryhill Township were purchased by Thomas McDonald, William Williams and Brawley Oates as trustees of the "Big Spring Campground of the Methodist Episcopal Church." By 1836 a "harbor" (brush arbor) had been constructed at the campground. The harbor had been built by David Kistler, a class leader (presumably of the Big Spring congregation), who regularly attended

*Frame church erected by Big Spring in 1907, torn down and replaced by the current brick church in 1953.*

the circuit meetings. But his bill for the work stirred some debate and took several years to resolve. Originally he'd offered to build it for $160, but he later submitted a bill for $297.67. An initial motion to pay him the full amount was rejected by the circuit, and a new group of trustees was named to reach a settlement with Mr. Kistler.

When Big Spring was formally organized as a church in 1866, the charter membership consisted of 33 men and 58 women. Evidently a church building was begun almost immediately. In June 1867 a committee was elected to finish the structure. A history of the church quotes from minutes of a Building Committee meeting on May 15, 1868, stating that Annanias Sing had proposed to "tongue and groove the planks and lay the floors, to make the seats with solid backs, build ceiling, close the upper windows, build pulpit and altar, put in lights, make sash, make and hang doors, all to be done in substantial and workable like manner. Work to be concluded 16th of August, 1868, for 20 acres of the land."

Despite its promising start and long history, Big Spring went into decline. In 1903 it was combined in a charge with Dilworth Church. The following year its membership numbered a mere 20 souls. In 1913 the Dilworth Church became a station and Big Spring, no longer paired with Dilworth, ceased to have a regular pastoral appointment. But the little church never closed its doors, kept alive by the dedication of two families–those of Dolph Freeman and David Sing.

Even in dark times hope prevailed. In 1907 a new frame church was built, at a cost of $1,300. By 1923, with a new supply pastor named J. A. Smith, the future began to brighten. Membership began to grow again, reaching 50 in 1929, with 86 persons enrolled in Sunday School. In 1935 a parsonage was built on the church property, and the congregation became self-supporting. In 1953, having outgrown the frame building, the congregation purchased a tent for $111, where worship was held while a new brick sanctuary was erected, much of the labor being donated by members. In 1960 the old parsonage was replaced by a new brick home. In 1980 Big Spring became part of a charge with Purcell Methodist.

In 2003 Big Spring became host to a new fellowship, the Ghana Community Mission Church, formed by the Rev. Emmanuel Yiadom, a member of Big Spring since 1998. The group meets at Big Spring Church.

New challenges have come with expansion of the nearby Charlotte-Douglas International Airport, and the encroachment of industrial enterprises. Despite a loss of members through death and transfer, Big Spring added seven new members in 2002, and looks forward in faith while recalling with justifiable pride a history of nearly 200 years.

# Blair Road UMC

Blair Road United Methodist Church had its beginning in September 1958 when the Rev. Robert Poindexter, Jr., a lay preacher then associated with Aldersgate Methodist, was asked by Bishop Nolan B. Harmon to investigate the possibilities of a new church in the Mint Hill area. Almost immediately a gathering was organized, and a service was held on September 26, 1958, in the home of W. A.

Elliotte, Jr. Later the group moved to the home of P. C. Williams, who had a large room suitable for worship services.

By October 20, 1958, a building had been rented. On February 1, 1959, Blair Road Church was formally established with 30 charter members. Officiating were Dr. Walter Miller, superintendent of the Charlotte District, and the Rev. Glenn Lackey, executive secretary of the Charlotte District Mission Society. The Rev. Poindexter became the first pastor.

The new congregation's first permanent building was erected in 1960 on a three-acre tract on Blair Road. The first service there was held on July 10 of that year. A parsonage was built in 1965, and a new sanctuary in 1972. An education building was added in 1981, and a newer one was completed in 2001.

*Blair Road United Methodist Church, about 1981, a pen and ink drawing by*
*Blair Road member Marcus Hamilton. Mr. Hamilton's work is better known in*
*another context: Since 1994 he has been drawing the daily Dennis The Menace*
*comic panel, published in major newspapers across the country.*
*He graciously consented to the use of this print in this book.*
*Dennis The Menace © Hank Ketcham Enterprises, Inc.*

# Calvary UMC

Calvary United Methodist Church was the second Methodist church to be started within the original Charlotte city limits. It began as a mission effort of Tryon Street Church under the leadership of the Rev. John F. Butt, a lay preacher who later became an ordained minister. Mr. Butt was a leader in Methodist expansion in Charlotte, helping form several churches in addition to Calvary. After starting Calvary, he went on to serve another church nearby, the Graham Street ME Church, South, and was instrumental in founding the Atherton Church, forerunner of Dilworth UMC.

Calvary was established in an area of Charlotte known for its rowdy gold miners. In his detailed history of the church, *A Century of Service,* George Dooley relates the story of revival services which launched the church. They were held at the home of Nick Smith, near a railroad crossing on Mint Street. Rev. Butt and his son, Arthur, led in singing to draw a crowd. Lanterns were hung from trees in the yard, and the front porch served as a pulpit. But it seems that not all those attracted to the proceedings were in a reverent mood. Mr. Butt says eggs and fruit were thrown at the worshippers.

The Church's first location was a small one-room building on South Mint Street at Morehead in 1865, where it remained about six years. But by the late 1800s, it had moved to the 600 block of South Church Street, in the area now occupied by the Charlotte Observer parking deck. The lot was donated by the Rev. W. S. Haltom, a retired minister and member of Tryon Street Church. Charlotte city directories for the late 1800s show the church was in a building at 614½ South Church Street. The property next door at 616 South Church served as a parsonage.

Trustees of the church in 1896 included G. M. Holobaugh, J. W. Tyzzer, George J. Etheridge, R. E. Holder, and J. J. Shuman. Mr. Shuman joined the church in 1867, and remained a stalwart member until his death in 1949, at the age of 96. The church has no written records prior to 1873, and much of its early story is based on information provided by Mr. Shuman.

Over the years the church has been known by different names. Originally it was known as the Calvary Mission Church. This name appears in an 1879 Charlotte City Directory, which lists the address as "S. Church near Hill Street." (The 600 block of South Church is between Stonewall and a smaller street known in those days as Hill Street.) Later city directories refer to it as "Church Street Methodist Episcopal Church, South," but revert to "Calvary Methodist Episcopal Church, South," about 1900. An entry dated April 13, 1900, in the Mecklenburg County Register of Deeds office refers to "Trustees, Church Street Methodist Episcopal Church South, now Calvary."

In 1934 Calvary moved to 1301 South Mint Street, and in 1952 relocated to its present home at 512 West Boulevard.

# Central UMC

You may wonder why a church on Albemarle Road, five miles from the center of Charlotte, would be named "Central United Methodist." The answer is simple enough: When they began on March 31, 1913, their first home was on Central Avenue. The church started with a small group of Christians holding worship services in the showroom of a Charlotte roofing company. As their number grew, they moved into a tent. By 1916 the new congregation had completed a

*Central United Methodist Church on Albemarle Road*

handsome brick sanctuary at 1201 Central Avenue, at the corner of Hawthorne Lane. Membership stood at 67. In time Sunday School rooms and educational facilities were added.

Until 1939 the congregation was known as First Methodist Protestant Church, part of a denomination which had split from the Methodist Episcopal Church in 1830. In 1939 the Methodist Protestant Church rejoined the Methodist Episcopal Church and the Methodist Episcopal Church, South, to form the Methodist Church. After the merger, the church took the name Central Avenue Methodist, from its location on Central Avenue.

By 1966, Central was attracting more than 500 persons for Sunday worship.

But in the late 1960s, as commercial enterprises began to crowd the church property, attendance fell, and the church decided to look for a new home. The Charlotte District Mission Society donated ten acres for a new building on Albemarle Road. On July 27, 1969, the last service was held in the old building. For the next year and a half Central's members held services at Memorial UMC, also on Central Avenue. On January 10, 1971, they moved into their new sanctuary. A month later the new Educational Building was consecrated. Membership, which had declined during the moving period, came back in strength, and within a decade attendance was setting new records. In 1986 the congregation occupied a new sanctuary, incorporating the old cornerstone carefully removed years earlier from the original building on Central Avenue. The little group no longer meets on that corner of Hawthorne and Central, but as a history of the church states, "The spirit of Christian love that founded the church has been preserved and cultivated. Children, young people and adults still find at Central United Methodist the caring and support that once caused it to be called the 'friendly church on the corner.'"

# Christ UMC

Early in 1959 five residents of the newly developed Coulwood community gathered at the home of Mr. and Mrs. Craig Lawing for a meeting that would lead to the creation of a new church. Taking part, in addition to Mr. Lawing, were Charles Dixon, Doyle Lakey, Jack Mock, Henry Mozeley, and the Rev. Glenn Lackey of the City Mission Society. In June of that year the Rev. George Rudisill was appointed to lead the new congregation, which began with 53 members.

Their first service was held July 19, 1959 in the Coulwood Community Building. Some 15 months later their first building was erected, a combination educational building and sanctuary, designed so that the sanctuary space could later be converted to classrooms. A new sanctuary was completed in 1969, and a Family Life Center was added in 1995.

# Cokesbury UMC

Cokesbury United Methodist Church dates its beginning from June 1958 when the appointment of its first pastor, the Rev. George Winecoff, was announced at the Annual Conference. Mr. Winecoff was a preacher without a church—no congregation, no building, not even a parsonage to live in. After three months of recruiting, 35 prospective members met on September 14 at the Methodist Home to organize the church. They elected officers and adopted a budget of $241 for the rest of the year.

A lot had been purchased by the Charlotte District Mission Society at the corner of Holbrook and Sharon Amity Road in preparation for starting the church. On September 28, 1958, members broke ground for their first building. By December, though still unfinished, the building was far enough along that the congregation was able to hold a service in it. The walls were unpainted, the floor was bare, there were no pews and no pulpit. A blanket of snow covered the ground outside. Yet three new members joined that cold wintry day, bringing the total number to 40. In the same month the church bought a parsonage on Amity Place. The price was $18,500.

Later an education building was added and renovations were made to the sanctuary. Still, as membership grew, Cokesbury needed more space, and in 1972 a new building was started on Idlewild Road. It was consecrated on November 18, 1973. In the following years a new parsonage was purchased, and a multipurpose building and fellowship hall were added, along with renovations to the sanctuary, kitchen and office areas.

Cokesbury has matured into an active, involved and mission-oriented church. Its Scout building was renovated for the Adult Care and Share program, which provides adult day care for elderly

*Cokesbury United Methodist Church*

and handicapped citizens. Its members participate in numerous projects including Habitat for Humanity and work teams that helped rebuild after hurricanes Andrew and Floyd.

# Cole Memorial UMC

Cole Memorial UMC traces its history back to 1891 when a Charlotte blacksmith and local preacher, George Page, established a preaching place in the Derita community. The congregation was organized as Derita Methodist Church in 1905. Land for their first building was donated by John Hunter, a member of Sugaw Creek Presbyterian Church. At first the church was part of a circuit with other Methodist churches, but in the late 1930s it became a "station." In 1938 the Rev. E. O. Cole became pastor and led the church into a

*Cole Memorial UMC*

period of growth. The church would later be named in his honor.

In 1939 the original wooden building was moved to the back of the property where it was brick veneered for use as an education building. A new sanctuary, still used today, was erected in front of it. In succeeding years a new education building was erected and, in 1974, a gymnasium was added. In the late 1980s a new parsonage was built.

# Commonwealth UMC

Commonwealth Methodist is one of several churches organized after the end of World War II under the sponsorship of the Charlotte District Mission Society. Seventeen people attended its first service, held in a tent, on June 23, 1946. On September 22 the church was officially organized, with the Rev. Robert H. Stamey as its first pastor. The tent was destroyed in a storm in October 1946, and the congregation moved to Midwood School.

Land had been purchased by the Mission Society, and the church's first permanent structure, now known as the Lands Building, was erected. It was used for Sunday School and worship services until classroom space in the main building was finished in 1948. The new sanctuary was completed in January 1951. The fellowship hall was added in 1957.

When the charter membership roll was closed on Easter Sunday 1947, 100 persons had joined. By 1972 membership stood at 641.

# Covenant UMC

Covenant United Methodist Church was formed in 1972 by the merger of Tuckaseegee Road and Wesley Heights churches.

Wesley Heights Church traces its history to 1883, when a small group of residents in the Seversville community formed the nondenominational Seversville Church. It later became Seversville Methodist, on a circuit with Pleasant Grove and Trinity Methodist churches. Originally the small congregation met in a public school building, but in 1902 they erected a building on Duckworth Avenue. In 1923 the church was renamed Duckworth Memorial, honoring Mr. and Mrs. Henry Duckworth, who had donated property for the building. In 1927 another new building was raised on Grandin Road and the name was changed again, to Wesley Heights Methodist Church. The church continued to grow, reaching a peak of more than 600 members.

Meanwhile, another group of westside residents, nine families in all, began meeting for worship under the leadership of the Rev.

*Former Tuckaseegee Road Methodist Church. The smaller building on the right was the original church, now called the Crane Building.*

Douglas R. Beard. Their first meeting was in May 1959 at the home of Mr. and Mrs. Joe McMurry, prime movers in organizing the new congregation. Soon they moved to an auction building, formerly an old airplane hangar, at the corner of Tuckaseegee and Ashley Roads, but as the cold of winter set in, they moved to warmer surroundings in the home of Mr. and Mrs. Henry Crane, Sr. Rev. Beard conducted worship in the living room. Bedrooms, den and kitchen were used for Sunday School classes. On August 9, 1959, they were organized officially as Tuckaseegee Road Methodist Church, with a membership of 40 persons. The following year, with help from the Charlotte District Mission Society, their first permanent building was completed. It included space for a temporary sanctuary and five classrooms. In 1966 the church began work on a two-unit, 13-room educational building. About the same time, another structure, now known as the Crane Building, was purchased from a nearby Presbyterian church and moved to the site. A new sanctuary was completed in 1973.

As 1970 drew to a close, Tuckaseegee Methodist had grown to about 250 members, but changing neighborhood patterns had begun to impact the larger Wesley Heights Church, once serving more than 600 persons. With its numbers declining, Wesley Heights approached Tuckaseegee about a merger. Following several meetings the two congregations voted to combine. A service of merger was held at Wesley Heights on May 2, 1971, and they were officially joined on June 6, 1971, meeting at Tuckaseegee. At that time a new name was adopted: Covenant United Methodist Church.

# Davidson UMC

Davidson College was founded in 1837, and the town of Davidson later grew up around it. The Davidson Methodist Church began about 1906, a Methodist outpost in a Presbyterian enclave. It is believed that Rev. W. H. Willis, pastor of Mount Zion Church in nearby Cornelius, played a leading role in starting the new congregation.

Founding members represented the "working people" of Davidson, including employees of a local asbestos plant and zipper factory, as well as nearby textile mills. It is said that for years, college professors were unable to join because the college required them to be practicing Presbyterians. In the late 1950s the rule was rescinded and by 1960 the congregation included more than 20 Davidson professors.

*Davidson UMC's restored Chapel Building*

The first building was a modest brick church on South Main Street, constructed of brick made locally in H. J. Brown's brickyard. The land was donated by J. L. Sloan. Members raised $1000 among themselves to pay for it and borrowed $500 more. The building was dedicated February 22, 1908. Later a fellowship hall was added which included a small kitchen. It came to be known as "the hut."

In 1960 a new building was erected across the street, and the original church was bought by a funeral home next door. Over the years the old building served as a funeral chapel, as temporary quarters for start-up churches, and eventually was converted into apartments.

In 2000 Davidson UMC decided to repurchase the old building and restore it to church use. Completely renovated, the little chapel was placed back into service in June 2003.

# Dilworth UMC

In 1891, developer Edward D. Latta launched his ambitious plans for Charlotte's first suburb, bestowing upon it his middle name, Dilworth. Not long thereafter a Methodist preacher named John F. Butt built the first church in the neighborhood. Mr. Butt, a supply pastor assigned to the City Mission Charge, had been leading prayer services in private homes. According to tradition, Butt, sensing the need for a place dedicated to worship, used his own funds to build a small wooden building at the corner of Cleveland and Worthington Avenues.

Records on file at the Mecklenburg Register of Deeds office show that the trustees of Charlotte's future uptown Trinity Church were involved with Methodist expansion into Dilworth, even before the Trinity Church itself was fully established.

On March 28, 1896, the trustees of the new Trinity Church, "holding property for Atherton Methodist Episcopal Church South in Dilworth, near Charlotte," bought a lot At Worthington and Cleveland Avenues from B. D. Heath. (Nineteen years later the same Mr. Heath would donate land for another new "suburban" church, Hawthorne Lane Methodist in the Elizabeth neighborhood.) The Trinity trustees identified in the deed were M. C. Mayer, Walter Brem, D. M. Rigler, M. L. Frazier, and R. N. Littlejohn, all former members of Tryon Street church.

An indenture recorded the following January (1897) by the same Trinity trustees refers to "a house of worship recently built." This document acknowledges a $150 "conditional donation" from the Board of Church Extension of the Methodist Episcopal Church South, Louisville, Kentucky, and pledges the lot and church as security for the "conditional donation." According to church tradition, the conference investment was essentially a reimbursement to Rev. Butt for the construction costs. At that time the name was changed to Dilworth Methodist Episcopal Church, South. The new congregation became part of a charge which included the uptown Trinity Church.

Originally the new house of worship was known as Atherton Church, taking its name from the nearby Atherton textile mill. James A. "Jim" Jones, a Methodist brickmason who would later found J. A. Jones Construction Company, built the brick piers and chimneys without charge for the first one-room building. Many years later the church named its educational building in his honor.

The first building faced Worthington Avenue. In 1913 work began on a new building which faced Cleveland Avenue. It was completed the following year. Dilworth experienced substantial growth in 1922 when a number of members transferred from Trinity and Tryon Street churches. This prompted discussion about a new building, which gained impetus with the promise by James B. Duke of $50,000 toward construction. In 1926 the imposing new church on East Boulevard was completed. The old building was sold to the First Church of the Nazarene.

Dilworth has enthusiastically served its community over the years. It established the Relatives, a runaway/crisis shelter for young adults, and served as the first home of Crisis Assistance Ministry. Today it continues as an active and committed congregation in the neighborhood that was Charlotte's "first streetcar suburb."

# Duncan Memorial UMC

Duncan Memorial began as a Sunday School class, organized in 1901 by members of nearby Brevard Street Methodist (now Memorial United Methodist Church). There were six children, representing two families in that first class. The Sunday School would continue for ten years before the church was formally established. It came into being on March 2, 1911, at which time it was named for the late Bishop William Wallace Duncan. Highland Park Manufacturing Company, which had previously provided space for Spencer Memorial Methodist, now allowed the new church to share space in a school building which it owned. The school eventually closed, and the church continued to use the building for 40 years. Highland Park later donated the building to the church. Proceeds from its sale helped finance a long-awaited new building.

From the beginning the congregation had dreamed of having a permanent sanctuary. In 1945 fundraising efforts began, highlighted by what became an annual fish fry. The Charlotte District Mission Society promised to help, and members of four large churches–First Methodist, Dilworth, Hawthorne Lane and Myers Park–also contributed. W. J. Edwards was named to head the committee soliciting from the four churches. A contract was negotiated which allowed members to donate materials and labor, saving a substantial amount on the building cost. The handsome colonial style edifice was completed in February 1951.

Duncan Memorial helped start one of Charlotte's first ethnic fellowships, the Cambodian Mission. It started about 1981 when Pastor Wade Rogers and church members took an interest in Cambodian refugee children in Optimist Park. The District Council on Ministries became involved, and, in 1990, formed a group called ReachOut. Funds were secured from the Conference Committee on Ethnic Local Church Concerns and Conference Council on Ministries to create a staff position and support the program.

A Cambodian congregation was formed, as well as a Hmong group. The Cambodian Mission now meets at First UMC. First Hmong, now officially a church, is mentioned below.

# First Hmomg UMC

First Hmong United Methodist Church is another of the ethnic congregations established in Charlotte in recent years with help from a group known as ReachOut.

Originally, the First Hmong Church met at First UMC on North Tryon Street, but now meets at Hickory Grove UMC. Recently they have acquired property through the Charlotte District Mission Society, and are planning to build their own sanctuary.

# First UMC

First United Methodist Church was formed in 1927 from the merger of Tryon Street and (uptown) Trinity churches. The Tryon Street church traces its roots to the original Methodist "class" organized in Charlotte in 1818 by Dr. David Dunlap. The history of "First Church" is treated in more detail in Chapter 12.

# Good Shepherd UMC

As with many new Methodist churches, Good Shepherd UMC had a pastor before there was a church. The Rev. Claude Kayler was appointed to serve the proposed congregation in June 1990. Land had been purchased by the Charlotte District the previous year, and the Rev. Kayler lost little time in recruiting his flock. A telemarketing and direct mail campaign in January 1991 was followed by the first worship service on February 10. It was held at Kennedy Junior High School. The church was officially constituted on May 19, 1991. In June they moved to the Olympic High School auditorium.

Direct mail continued to be an effective tool in drawing new members. On one Sunday in September 1994, 34 new families came to Good Shepherd as a result of direct mail. By February 1996 the growing congregation was in its first permanent building, located at 13110 Moss Road. The church began a preschool later that year.

A youth outreach program called "Rush Hour" was launched in September 1999, and a year later it was expanded to two nights. An education building was completed in June 2000. Attendance had

*Good Shepherd United Methodist Church*

grown to the point that by September 2000 the church was holding three morning worship services. In January 2004, with worship attendance now reaching more than 900, the church broke ground for a third building, which will include a worship center and additional classrooms.

# Grace UMC

Like the circuit riders of old, the Rev. Robert Crowley was sent forth in September 1953 to create a new church where one had not existed before. His salary, temporarily, was to be paid by Dilworth Methodist Church, which also agreed to furnish a parsonage. Other funds came from the Charlotte District Mission Society.

The field of labor was on the south side of Charlotte, and his new appointment was identified simply as the "South Charlotte Church."

On November 8 the first service was held in the auditorium of Park Road Elementary School, with arrangements being handled by Charlie Davis and Ward Hinkle. Forty persons attended church school and 87 were there for the worship service. Mr. Hinkle would become the first Church School superintendent. Three weeks later the name "Grace Methodist" was selected for the new church.

Land for a church building was donated by Judge and Mrs. D. E. Henderson. Additional land was purchased in the following months. On February 6, 1955, the groundbreaking for the new building was held in a pouring rain.

The building was completed in time for services to be held in it on Mother's Day, May 8. That building is now the fellowship hall. Within another year the children's building, now known as the Brown Building or Scout Building, opened. Planning soon began for a sanctuary building. The groundbreaking was held in 1959. It was completed and the first service held in it on Mother's Day in May 1961.

In 2003 the church celebrated its 50th anniversary. A booklet prepared to mark the occasion concludes, "Grace United Methodist

Church is trying in every way to meet the needs of and minister to the congregation and to the community at large. Surely God has a real purpose in establishing Grace Church, and it is with a firm belief and trust that He will lead this church into and throughout the future. We pray that God will help us to become the church He wants us to be."

## Greater Vision UMC

Greater Vision UMC is one of the newest churches in the Charlotte District, having started in 2003. Discussions regarding establishment of the new church began in April 2003. The Rev. Alexis Anthony was appointed pastor at the Annual Conference in June of that year, to serve what was called the "Northeast Mecklenburg Mission."

In July a group of interested people was called together to begin making plans for forming a congregation. The Rev. Nancy Rankin of University City UMC assisted with plans for a meeting space. A core group of prospective members was assembled and began a seven-week series of meetings on Methodist heritage and the purpose of forming a new church.

Three names were proposed for the church: Genesis, New Jerusalem and Greater Vision. By majority vote, members selected the name, Greater Vision. Their first worship as a group came as part of a revival at Burge Memorial UMC in Mount Holly. On November 30, 2003, Greater Vision held its first worship service as a congregation, with more than 150 persons in attendance. The congregation meets at University City UMC.

## Harrison UMC

Harrison United Methodist Church is acknowledged to be the oldest existing Methodist congregation in Charlotte, although the precise date of its beginning has not been determined. The generally accepted date is 1785, when a small group of worshippers gathered for services conducted by their own leaders and occasionally by a visiting circuit rider. The church's traditional beginning dates from a reference in minutes of the old Santee Circuit of South Carolina, in the year 1815. More about Harrison Church can be found in an earlier chapter of this book.

# Hawthorne Lane UMC

Hawthorne Lane Methodist Episcopal Church, South, was established in 1915 by members of Tryon Street, Trinity (uptown) and a sprinkling of transfers from Calvary Methodist, which at that time was also located uptown. Prominent Charlotte businessmen J. B. Ivey, B. D. Heath, and E. A. Cole were among the founders, although a committee of Methodist women, Mrs. Charles Stone, Mrs. S. J. Asbury and Mrs. C. O. Brown, is credited with initiating the effort. Many of the original members lived in or near the emerging Elizabeth neighborhood where the church is located. Among their number were Ivey, who lived just over the hill at 418 Central Avenue, Heath, just a block from the Iveys, and Cole, at 608 Central Avenue. Heath's Oakhurst Land Company donated land for the new church at Hawthorne Lane and Eighth Street.

Hawthorne Lane, previously named Kingston Avenue (the name was changed in 1914 to avoid confusion with a street of the same name in Dilworth), was something of an early belt road, linking the Piedmont neighborhood along Central Avenue with the Elizabeth development on the south side of what is now Independence Freeway. Over the hill, where Hawthorne Lane met Fourth Street, was the entrance to George Stephen's new housing development named Myers Park.

On November 17, 1915, at the Annual Conference in Shelby, Bishop Walter Lambuth appointed the Rev. Robert D. Sherrill to be the first pastor at Hawthorne Lane. Just two and a half weeks later, on December 5, Rev. Sherrill led the first service at Elizabeth Col-

*Hawthorne Lane UMC, as it looked in the 1940s*

lege, a former school for young women which was in the process of closing. (The college property later became the new home of Presbyterian Hospital.) *The Charlotte Observer* for Monday, December 6, reported the auditorium was completely filled. For its first year the congregation met at the college,

Louis Asbury, a young Charlotte architect who had studied at MIT, was selected to plan a building for the new church. His parents, Mr. and Mrs. S. J. Asbury, were charter members of the Hawthorne Lane congregation. A contract was let with J. A. Jones Construction Company on Feb. 12, 1916, to build a sanctuary with space for Sunday school rooms. The cost was $38,119. In December 1916, a year after its beginning, the church held its first service in its new building.

Across Hawthorne Lane from the church property was a large bungalow with a wraparound porch, formerly occupied by a young lawyer named Norman Cocke, destined to become president of Duke Power Company, and namesake for Lake Norman. The house was used for a time as a parsonage for the church, and many years later became the home of author Harry Golden.

The Education Building was added in 1925.

For many years Hawthorne Lane was one of the largest Methodist churches in Charlotte, with membership reaching a peak of more than 2,000. By the 1960s membership had begun to decline as

Charlotte's population stepped up its march to the suburbs, but as the 21st century dawned the church retained its leadership role as one of the district's most vigorous and recognized congregations.

# Hickory Grove UMC

Hickory Grove is one of the historic churches of Charlotte, tracing its roots to a fellowship of Wesley followers who started meeting in private homes, with worship led by circuit-riding preachers. In 1844 they organized Prospect Church, which would later become Hickory Grove.

John Maxwell deeded property to the congregation "on the waters of McAlpine Creek," but it would be another four years before their first meeting house was completed. Located on Delta Road (now Harris Boulevard) between Albemarle and Hickory Grove roads, it was a log cabin measuring 16 by 25 feet with four benches on each side of a single aisle and a window behind the pulpit. It is said the small church was one of only two in the state that had a stove for heating. This may account for it housing some of the first Sunday School classes held in the state.

On August 18, 1858, John Johnson deeded three acres to the Prospect congregation for a new sanctuary. It was on Pence Road about a mile from the first location, in a large grove of Hickory trees which would give the church its new name. The new building was 24 by 35 feet, still small by today's standards, but more than double the size of the first structure. In keeping with the Methodist custom, men and women were seated on opposite sides of the aisle. There were also separate amen corners for men and women.

Following the Civil War the church experienced new growth, and by 1898 a new building was needed. The new structure included two rooms at the front for Sunday School, and a bell tower. In 1915 Hickory Grove welcomed the Rev. M. I. Steel, a Civil War veteran nearing retirement. He was the first pastor in fulltime ministry appointed to Hickory Grove, though his services were shared with Derita and Newell.

*Hickory Grove UMC under construction, 1935*

Today's beautiful stone sanctuary was started in 1926, and took nearly ten years to complete. The basement was dug with shovels, plows and drag pans. The dirt was hauled out in wheelbarrows. Stones were quarried nearby and brought to the site in mule-drawn wagons. J. D. Pence, who had joined the church in 1871, over 50 years earlier, was a driving force in the project.

Mr. Pence was a man of devout faith. The story is told that during a prolonged drought, he attended a special meeting at which members planned to pray for rain. He brought his umbrella.

The stock market crash of 1929 cast a pall on fund raising for the new building. But with prayer, sweat and determination the work went forward. By the time of its dedication in 1935, the church and parsonage had been paid for in full. In an article in the *Christian Advocate,* the Rev. E. K. McLarty called it "the prettiest country church and community in this part of North Carolina." At the end of its first century, in 1944, the church had more than 800 members.

In 1959 the church launched a new building program which included an enlarged sanctuary, a contemporary narthex, new educational building, and chapel. An activity building was erected in 1975.

# Homestead UMC

Homestead Methodist Church was chartered in 1932, but grew from seeds which had been planted as much as a decade earlier. In the early 1920s a group of residents in Homestead Village, off Rozelles Ferry Road, organized a non-denominational Sunday School. At first they met in a vacant house, but later moved into the Leaksville Mills Community Building. Soon, ministers from nearby churches began holding occasional Sunday evening worship services there, and, in 1932, the Rev. Bryan Crosby, pastor of Chadwick Methodist Church, held a revival. A community survey revealed substantial interest in forming a new church, and on October 30, 1932, 92 persons became charter members of the new Homestead Church. The Rev. Carl H. King was appointed pastor, serving a two-point charge which included Duncan Memorial Church. In 1933 Homestead was paired with Pleasant Grove on a two-point charge, an arrangement which continued until 1948. The Rev. J. O. Ervin became Homestead's first fulltime pastor that year.

The congregation continued to meet in the Community Building until a sanctuary was built in 1958. Their first service in the new building was held on January 25, 1959. A multipurpose building was added in 1971, with the men of the church donating hundreds of hours of labor for all of the inside woodwork. A bell tower was erected in 1975, financed largely from memorials and ham suppers held by the Methodist Men.

# Hunters Chapel UMC

On October 12, 2003, Hunters Chapel United Methodist Church celebrated 94 years of service to the Lord with a ceremony attended by five of their past ministers and three former members who were called to the ministry.

One of Mecklenburg's oldest Methodist churches, Hunters Chapel erected its first building in 1909, on land donated by the

Gillespie family. That original building was faced with plank board, and sat on a leaning rock foundation. The floor sloped toward the front. A church history comments that anyone entering the back on roller skates could coast down to the front of the church. It is not recorded if anyone actually did this. At first, the building had only one door, at the front. Later, a second door was added. The ceiling was high, allowing the hot air of summer to rise above the congregation. A pot bellied stove in the center of the sanctuary kept worshippers warm in the winter. Lanterns provided light for night services. The first electric lights were installed in 1938, by Roy Alexander. New stained glass windows were purchased in 1978. The bell which now hangs in the steeple was originally supported by a pole in front of the church.

Older members recall that the original church was in a valley, so that on rainy days cars would get stuck in the mud trying to leave. Men would muddy their good Sunday clothes pushing cars up the hill after church. Everyone knew of a place not to sit on rainy days, because the roof overhead had a leak.

In 1960 when Duke Power was clearing land for Lake Norman, it bought the old church and a new structure was built on the present site, on John Connor Road, in the "Peninsula" area near Lake Norman. Graves from the old cemetery were also moved.

*The new Hunters Chapel UMC building, erected in 1961*

Hunters Chapel describes itself as a small, family oriented congregation, the only minority United Methodist church in Mecklenburg County outside the city of Charlotte. It is a church filled with memories for many descendants of the original founders, and a place of peace and joy for its present members.

# Huntersville UMC

Huntersville UMC had a very ecumenical beginning. When the congregation first assembled in 1901, it shared space (and even preachers) with a Baptist church, and both churches used a building borrowed from a Presbyterian church. The Methodists and Baptists met in an old wooden sanctuary belonging to the Huntersville Associate Reformed Presbyterian Church, where their ministers conducted services on alternating Sundays. Two years later both congregations moved out, to a new location which they again shared. Now it was called the Anchor Mill Mission, actually in a former mill house. The two churches held Sunday School at the same time, followed by a joint worship service. The Methodist and Baptist preachers took turns leading the service.

The Methodist minister, the Rev. Marvin Hoyle, drew plans for a church building, but it still had not been constructed at the time of his death. Eighteen years after their founding, in 1919, the congregation completed their own sanctuary. It would be another ten years before an addition to provide new Sunday School rooms would be completed.

The church struggled for many years, sharing the services of a pastor with other churches on a multi-point charge. At various times these included Mt. Zion, Asbury and Oak Grove churches. In the 1940s, with Sunday services being held in the afternoon, attendance declined to the point that sometimes as few as five or six persons were present.

In 1946, facing the possible death of the church, members were relieved when William McLendon, an ordained deacon, volunteered to serve as a supply pastor. But then his health failed, and for six years the church was served by a succession of student preachers from Davidson College. In 1954, the church again received a supply pastor, the Rev. Hugh Simms, and attendance began to grow. Within a year membership reached 107. Regular pastoral appointments resumed in 1957, and the church continued to grow. In 1961 the congregation moved to a new building, now called the Argo Chapel, at their present site. By 1962 attendance had doubled, and adjoining property was purchased for a parking lot and expansion. In 1978 the first phase of a new educational building was erected, and in 1986 the present sanctuary was completed. In 1987 the church was able to participate in a community ministry by providing space for the Huntersville Food Pantry. The Argo Chapel was later renovated to provide larger quarters for the food pantry, additional Sunday School classrooms and a prayer room.

As this book goes to press, the church has purchased the land for a new sanctuary, and plans were being made for a facility on that site.

# Kilgo UMC

Kilgo Methodist Church was organized with 37 members on September 5, 1943, one of the first two churches (along with St. John's) established through efforts of the new Charlotte District Mission Society. Its mission: to serve the fast growing neighborhoods in Charlotte's Plaza-Midwood area. The church is named for Bishop John C. Kilgo, who presided at the Western North Carolina Annual Conference in 1916 and who once had a home in the area.

For more than a year, morning services were held at Midwood School, with night services and other activities at the church parsonage. In 1944 the stately former residence of J. C. McNeill was acquired for use as a sanctuary by the Mission Society. Four years later the church erected its first new building, a fellowship hall, at a cost of $10,000.

*J. C. McNeill residence, first home of Kilgo United Methodist Church*

In 1950, Kilgo completed a successful campaign to raise funds for a new sanctuary, but then members decided an education building should be erected first. This building was completed in 1954. The McNeill house continued to serve the church as a sanctuary until a new sanctuary was completed in October 1960.

Even while members were busy with the church's own building program, they never lost sight of a more important goal of missionary outreach. Individuals and Sunday School classes adopted Korean orphans, sponsored schooling for Indian boys, and helped finance a much needed Indian well. Local, district and worldwide missions have always been a part of the outreach at Kilgo Church.

# Light of Christ UMC

The Rev. Maria Hanlin, the first pastor of Light of Christ UMC, tells a remarkable story of how the church started. It began when she was an associate at Matthews UMC. In her account, the Rev. Ken

Lyon, senior pastor at Matthews, said he believed God wanted her to start a new church in Ballantyne in southeast Charlotte. Maria's dream, however, had been to work with poor families in the inner city. She resisted, telling Ken, "If God wants me to start a new church, he'll send the pastor of that new church, Christ Church at Ballantyne, to my door tomorrow."

Incredibly, it happened almost that way. The following morning, while attending a breakfast at McAlpine Elementary School, she shared a table with a stranger who turned out to be Jeff Gardner, pastor of Christ Church at Ballantyne.

Later in the same week, Rev. Lyon showed Maria a doctoral paper written by a pastor neither of them knew, Dana McKim. McKim had done a study, concluding that a new church was needed in southeast Charlotte; that it should be started by an existing church (he suggested Matthews UMC), and ideally would be started by the associate pastor at Matthews. McKim's recommendation even profiled the ideal candidate to start the new church—someone in his or her 30s, with two children, and live near Ballantyne Common Parkway. The description matched Maria exactly.

After much prayer, God's plan for the church began to unfold in Maria's mind. It would be "a place where people of any background, every color, would be welcomed; a church that would reach out to the hurting, the divorced, the single parents, the addicted, the poor, those who had lost hope, those whose lives were spinning out of control."

Finally, Maria answered the call and Light of Christ began to take shape. Its mission, she says, is not to simply move people from other congregations, but to "find the stray sheep," people not being served by an existing church. To attract kids "of all sizes" the church provides doughnuts and hot chocolate. They have a praise band. The service is geared to people who may feel uncomfortable with "churchy music" and ministers in robes using "17th century language."

In January 1999, a small group began meeting monthly to worship and plan for the new church. A series of obstacles threatened the project, but each one was swept aside, almost as if by miracle. On

October 4, weekly Sunday morning worship began at William Davies Park on Highway 51. They soon outgrew the facilities, and moved in November to the new Hawk Ridge Elementary School. Within two years membership had grown from an original 27 to 239, with an average attendance of 350 at Sunday worship. In the year 2000 Light of Christ purchased property on Bryant Farms Road. A small house on the property serves as church offices and includes two small meeting rooms. The congregation currently meets for Sunday worship at Jay Robinson Middle School, but has plans for a permanent building some day on their property on Bryant Farm Road.

# Matthews UMC

In 1877 a group of about 20 persons left the old Fairview Methodist Church on Weddington-Matthews Road to form a new church in the town of Matthews. Later the Fairview Church was disbanded, and its remaining members joined the Matthews Church.

Joseph McLaughlin gave the new church a lot to build on at the corner of Ames and Charles Streets in Matthews. The deed for the seven-eighths acre site was dated September 8, 1877. The first structure was a small, frame, one-room sanctuary. Initially it was on a circuit with Hickory Grove, Zion, and Little Bethel (Stouts). The different congregations supported each other, and the Matthews Church was able to pay for digging a well through contributions from the Hickory Grove Church. The story is told that Hickory Grove later asked to be repaid for the well. A member of the Matthews congregation is said to have replied, "We don't have the money. Come get the well."

In 1903 the first building was demolished and a new wooden building erected, later to be brick veneered. Its foyer had separate entrances to the left and right side of the sanctuary. According to early custom, men would enter and sit on the left; women would sit on the right. An exception was made for newly-married couples, who would sit together on the women's side.

*Two early buildings used by Matthews UMC. Top: the first church, built in 1877; bottom: the second building, erected in 1903.*

Over the years Matthews was teamed with different churches on varying circuits, and several times was a station, with its own pastor. In 1939 it permanently became a one-church station, or charge.

As the church grew, its aging building needed replacement, and in 1959 a new sanctuary was completed. It served for 30 years, until the members voted, in 1989, to build again. This time, they decided to move to a new location, on Trade Street west of Matthews School. A handsome structure was completed on that site, and today continues to serve a growing and active congregation.

# Memorial UMC

In 1888 a mission was established by the Tryon Street Church which would become Brevard Street Methodist. Members began meeting in a small three-room house on Alexander Street, between Seventh and Eighth Streets in First Ward.

From the beginning the mission was a success. Within a few years the congregation became too large for the small house and, about 1894, a lot was acquired on North Brevard Street, between 11th and 12th Streets. A wooden building was erected, but it, too, was soon outgrown. A new site was purchased at 614 North Brevard Street and in 1898 a Sunday School building was constructed. A house next door at 612 North Brevard was the parsonage. In 1905 the main church building was finished, and the name became Brevard Street Methodist Episcopal Church, South.

In 1907 the congregation numbered 509 members, then declined during World War I, but climbed again to a peak of 630 in 1942. In the late 1940s membership declined again as veterans returned from World War II and families moved to the suburbs. In 1950 the congregation voted to seek a new location. They found it in a six-acre site on Central Avenue, in a section then known as Albemarle Road. Ground was broken on November 8, 1953. While construction was underway the congregation, now numbering 330 members, held services on Sunday afternoons at Green Memorial Baptist Church.

With a new location the church needed a new name, and it became Memorial Methodist Church. The first service in the new building was held on March 21, 1954. Within eight months 76 new members were added.

In 1955 work began on a fellowship hall. In 1958 a new sanctuary was completed, and in 1965 a new educational wing was added.

# Moore's Chapel UMC

Before its official founding, Moore's Chapel had been known as Dow's, a name which has a long history in Mecklenburg County Methodism. According to minutes of quarterly meetings, there was a meeting place known as Dow's on the old Charlotte Circuit as early as 1846.

Moore's Chapel UMC, as we know it today, was formally organized in 1884, probably taking its name from M. M. Moore, who owned adjoining property. The meeting house was located near the Catawba River, close to the landing for a ferry which made the crossing between Mecklenburg and Gaston counties. In its early years it was paired on a circuit with the Ebenezer Methodist Church in Belmont.

# Morningstar UMC

Morningstar is one of Mecklenburg's newer churches, but has its roots in a much older congregation. Members of the former Steeleberry United Methodist Church began planning for the new Morningstar church in January 2001. Following the appointment of the Rev. Brad Thie as pastor of Steeleberry in June 2002, planning continued, with help from the Western North Carolina Conference Congregational Development office and the District Mission Society, as well as Good Shepherd and Providence United Methodist churches. The first worship service of the new church was held on Sunday, September 14, 2003. More than 100 people attended the service, held at Olympic High School. During the worship hour a children's ministry called JOY! (Jesus, Others, You) was started.

Information from the WNNC Archives indicates that Steeleberry UMC was itself the successor to another church, Morris Field. According to a history by G. W. Bumgarner, the Morris Field Church was organized in 1946-47.

# Mount Zion UMC

Zion Methodist Church was started in 1827 by Samuel Kerr, a brother of Margaret Kerr Martin, a founder of Buckhill/Trinity UMC. The deed was filed July 2, 1828 for a site one mile west of Cornelius on the present NC 73. The church was on this site until 1835, when property for a new church was donated by Alexander Johnson. The new site was on the Charlotte-Statesville Road in Cornelius. The name was changed from Zion to Mount Zion when the congregation moved to their new building. An interesting sidelight is that graves from the old church cemetery on Highway 73 were later moved to a special section known as the Community Cemetery at the new location to make way for a housing development.

Oldtimers recall that members of Mount Zion Church participated in organizing Davidson Methodist Church.

# Mouzon UMC

Mouzon Methodist Church held its first service on Sunday, November 28, 1943 in the parsonage of its pastor, the Rev. Roy E. Bell. The young Mr. Bell, less than a year out of seminary at Duke University, had been appointed a few months previously to organize a new church in the Selwyn Avenue area. Rev. Bell would later joke that Bishop Clare Purcell had appointed him to a tree on Selwyn Avenue.

Mouzon was the third church to be organized by the Charlotte City Mission Society, later renamed the Charlotte District Mission Society. The society purchased the parsonage, at 2842 Selwyn Avenue. Mrs. Edwin L. Jones, Sr., personally selected furnishings for the home and supervised the job of setting up the minister's new home.

Immediately after moving in, Rev. Bell began canvassing the neighborhood for prospective members. The first family to sign up was Mr. and Mrs. F. H. Tathwell, Jr.

The first service was held in the living room and adjacent dining room with 21 worshippers present, including the pastor and Mrs. Bell. Sunday School, which began the following Sunday, had classes in the living room, dining room, pastor's study and a vacant bedroom upstairs.

Mouzon Church was officially organized January 10, 1944. Dr. Edgar Nease, district superintendent, presided at the Monday evening meeting. Dr. Nease said the bishop had specifically asked the congregation not to name their church after a street. One of the first suggestions was to name the church for the Jones family, who had provided significant help in getting it started. Dr. Nease said the Jones family wished to stay in the background and, after further discussion, it was agreed to name the church in honor of Bishop Edwin DuBose Mouzon, considered one of Methodism's most able preachers and administrators.

# Myers Park UMC

When George Stephens developed the new streetcar suburb of Myers Park, one of the amenities he provided was a community store at the intersection of Providence and Queens Roads. That store was destined to become the first home of Myers Park Methodist Church.

The church began in 1925 with a meeting on the front porch of Myers Park resident Dr. R. T. Ferguson, when a few of the neighbors decided to form a new church. Those ten pioneers are still remembered by the church today: J. J. Akers, Fred Anderson, Louis H. Asbury, Robert I. Dalton, Dr. P. C. Hull, George H. Moore, H. C. Sherrill, W. Z. Stultz, D. D. Traywick and Dr. Ferguson.

The following day a committee consisting of three of the members, Akers, Stultz and Ferguson, met with the presiding elder (district superintendent), Dr. J. B. Craven, and obtained his approval to move ahead. They adopted a budget of $8,000, which the ten men pledged to contribute. For a pastor, they chose a dynamic young preacher, the Rev. Excelle Rozelle, who was then principal of the

Mount Holly Schools. He had been admitted to the conference several years earlier, but, because of a health problem, had not previously been appointed to a church. Now recovered, he was approved by Dr. Craven, and formally appointed at the 36th Annual Conference to serve the Myers Park church.

During the early stages of forming the church, eight other men joined the organizing committee, and their names deserve mention here. They were S. B. Tanner, Jr., F. W. Bradshaw, B. D. Heath, S. A. Ault, J. E. Sebrell, Jr., J. H. Frye, H. W. Cox, and R. L. Campbell.

The first service was held October 25, 1925, in the Queens College Chapel with 85 charter members. Within two months they had purchased the Community Store as their first permanent home, at a price of $18,000. Worship services were held in the store building for the first time on December 16, 1925. Sunday School was conducted upstairs in a space formerly used as a kindergarten. By the time the charter membership roll was closed on December 31, an-

*Myers Park Community Store at Providence and Queens Roads served as the first home of Myers Park United Methodist Church in 1925. It was moved in 1929 to make way for the new sanctuary and was later demolished.*

other 66 members had been added for a total of 151.

In 1930 the church completed the imposing Gothic-style edifice we see today at the intersection of Queens and Providence Roads. Its stone is from the same Hillsborough quarry that furnished stone for Duke University. It is thought that James B. Duke, whose Charlotte home was nearby, made arrangements for the stone shortly before his death in 1925.

Like many other churches, Myers Park Methodist struggled during the depression years of the early 1930s. Members of the Board of Trustees personally co-signed documents to refinance the church debt. Among the leaders during those difficult days was J. Luther Snyder, who served as chairman of the Board of Stewards from 1933 through 1935.

Among many members who have been gracious in their giving to the church, Mr. Snyder's generosity is especially noteworthy. An executive with Charlotte's Coca-Cola Bottling Company, he joined the church in 1930. Even before becoming a member, he presented the church a check for $10,000. In 1932 he contributed the bronze tablets on the front corners of the church. Four years later he gave a Hammond organ, replacing a theater organ contributed earlier by Warren Irvin. In March 1937 that he proposed his biggest gift of all–$100,000 for construction of a new educational building. Mr. Snyder explained that he had come to church one rainy Sunday to find children huddled under umbrellas inside their leaking classrooms. He added that he was concerned about fire safety in the old wooden "huts" used by the children. The magnificent Luther Snyder Memorial Educational Building opened in January 1938. Stone for it came from the same Hillsborough quarry as that used in the sanctuary. In 1953 Mr. Snyder pledged another $60,000 to enlarge the building.

The campaign to pay off the previous debt reached its goal in the spring of 1941. The sanctuary was formally dedicated on April 18, with Bishop Clare Purcell delivering the sermon.

Through the years, other additions have enhanced the facilities and programs of Myers Park Church. Stained glass windows and chimes were installed in the 1940s. In 1950 a new Aeolian-Skinner pipe organ was installed, at the time considered one of the finest organs in the Southeast. Ownbey Hall, named for former pastor Dr. Richard Ownbey, was completed during the 1950s renovations to the Snyder Building. In June 2003 a new Parish Life Building was consecrated, nearly doubling the size of the church complex. It was constructed of the same stone used in the earlier buildings.

As remarkable as Myers Park's physical facilities are, it is equally remarkable to note the enthusiasm devoted to financial support for mission work. Over the years members have contributed generously to the support of missionaries in Malaya, China, Pakistan and Africa; to the building of churches in India and Costa Rica; relief work following natural disasters in Nicaragua and Chile; outreach programs in Appalachia; and countless projects closer to home such as Habitat for Humanity and programs to relieve poverty and hunger.

# Oak Grove UMC

In 1888 about 16 members left Bethel Methodist Protestant Church to form a new church near Croft, a historic community now on the northern fringes of Charlotte. According to folklore, the separation may have stemmed from political differences—part of the congregation were Democrats; the other, Republicans. History did not record which group was the one which left.

Led by the Rev. Harper Christenbury, they raised a small one room building on property donated by Charlie and Ann Henderson, located on what is now NC 115, the Old Statesville Road. The church was named Oak Grove, from a grove of trees near the building. For more than a half century the little church served its members, although a member later recalled some Sunday School classes were held outside. She attended an elementary class that was held in a car. A young men's class used the back of a pickup truck.

As World War II drew to a close, with veterans returning and the prospect of new growth, discussions began on the need for a newer and larger building. Through the generosity of Mr. and Mrs. Bruce

*Oak Grove's first building*

Henderson a site was acquired at 6440 Old Statesville Road, where the present church is located. Work began in 1948. Before the new structure was finished a fire on Easter Sunday morning heavily damaged the old church building. Since the new one wasn't ready for use, the old one was repaired.

The basement portion of the new building was completed in time for a formal opening in June 1950, with a revival service conducted by the Rev. C. C. Benton. The following April the sanctuary was finished. The first service held in it was the wedding of Betty Griffin and Clarence Phillips. Mrs. Phillips today is the church historian.

Among the many interesting notes in the church's long history is that for two years, 1960-62, the pastor was a Norwegian, the Rev. Fridmann Rossborg.

Expansion of the church building, completed in 1997, added classroom space and made the building handicap-accessible.

Note: Historian G. W. Bumgarner shows Oak Grove existing earlier than 1888. However, he may have been thinking of the old Bethel Church, which preceded Oak Grove.

# Pineville UMC

Stories abound of cooperation and partnership between Methodists and Presbyterians in the formative years of Methodism in Mecklenburg County. Pineville United Methodist Church is an example.

The congregation that is now Harrison United Methodist Church, Mecklenburg's pioneer Methodist society, had formed less than four miles from what is now Pineville about 1785. The town of Pineville itself grew around a stop on the Charlotte, Columbia and Augusta Railway, completed in 1852. It would be another 15 years before the town would have a church of its own.

In 1867 a one-room schoolhouse was built on Johnston Drive. A group of Presbyterians sought permission to use the school as a place of worship, and soon they were joined by a group of Methodists. Nine years later, when the Presbyterians built their own church, the Methodists moved with them to the new building.

In 1879 the Methodists finally got their own building, on land donated by a member, Samuel Younts. According to a church history, Younts came to Pineville after serving in the Civil War. He set up a blacksmith shop, general store and livery stable. He invested in land and lent money to local farmers and businessmen. Bricks for the building were handmade with clay from the banks of Sugar Creek by Mr. Younts another member, Milas Yandle, who was a brickmaker

*Pineville Methodist Church, 1878*

by trade, and Yandle's son, Edward. The building was started under the leadership of the Rev. Lucius Edney Stacy, who had been appointed to the circuit a year earlier. Pineville was part of a circuit which included the Harrison and Hebron churches. Rev. Stacy travelled the circuit by horse and buggy.

Prominent among the early members was Dr. Joseph Alexander Ardrey. Dr. Ardrey was born in the Providence community in 1852, and graduated from the Medical College of Charleston. He practiced medicine throughout southern Mecklenburg County and upper South Carolina, making house calls by horse and buggy until his death in 1893.

The first Sunday School building was erected in 1930, to be replaced by the present Stacy Hall in 1958. The original sanctuary was torn down and replaced by the present structure in 1964.

Pineville remained part of a circuit until 1950, when the Rev. Mitchell Faulkner was appointed as its first full-time pastor.

# Plaza UMC

Plaza United Methodist Church had its beginning in 1960, when a group of 16 people from several churches came together in an effort to establish a new church on The Plaza, in northeast Charlotte. They began holding worship services at the Methodist Home. On May 21, 1961, the first service was held in their new sanctuary. The congregation grew rapidly, and by the mid 1970s there was discussion of building a new sanctuary. But after much debate, the congregation decided instead to invest in a new Family Life Center, which would include a chapel, gymnasium, kitchen, classrooms and office space.

Plaza Church has actively supported a variety of community-service programs, including the Plaza Adult Learning Services, a hot lunch program for senior citizens, Scouting, basketball leagues, Headstart, Loaves and Fishes, and the Plaza Performing Arts Ministry.

In 1994 Plaza UMC, a traditionally white church, took another pioneering step when it welcomed Dr. Percival Reeves, its first African-American minister. As demographics in the community shifted, the church responded. In a three-year period, 225 new members joined the congregation, making Plaza not only one of the fastest growing congregations in the Western North Carolina Conference, but the first new predominantly African American congregation in the conference in 25 years.

# Pleasant Grove UMC

According to tradition, Pleasant Grove Methodist Episcopal Church got its start as early as 1863, with a group of worshippers meeting in the log cabin home of Rachel Hutchinson. Later they moved to a brush arbor just west of the present Scout Hut. The church was formally established in June 1888 by the Rev. George Page. Mrs. Hutchinson donated the land where the first church building was built in 1889. It was described as being 21 x 40 feet, with wooden slabs for benches.

In 1908 the congregation constructed a second building across the road which was heated by two pot bellied stoves, one on each side of the pulpit. A third was erected in 1948 at the corner of Oakdale and Pleasant Grove Roads. Much of the work was done by members.

Originally Pleasant Grove was a part of a circuit, sharing the services of a pastor with Big Spring, Prospect/Hickory Grove, Trinity and Derita churches.

Today the congregation occupies a complex of buildings which includes a sanctuary building, children's education building, older adult education, offices and chapel, a gymnatorium and child day care center.

# Providence UMC

On November 29, 1953, Charlotte attorney Paul Ervin and Mrs. Ervin invited a group of friends to a Sunday evening prayer service at their home on Sharon Lane. More prayer meetings were held in the following weeks and, as more people began to attend, discussion turned to a more formal relationship. On January 10, 1954, they voted unanimously to form a new church. Ten couples agreed to become members.

On January 17, 1954, the first formal worship service of the yet-unnamed church was held in the Sharon School auditorium on Sharon Road. The Rev. Frank Jordan, Charlotte district superintendent, preached the first sermon.

As with any good Methodist group, the first order of business was to organize committees. George M. Ivey, Sr. became the first chairman of the Official Board. A member recalls that the board would meet over dinner at Thacker's Restaurant on South Tryon Street, where the meal cost $1.50.

Eight years previously, the Charlotte City Mission Society had purchased about four acres at the corner of Providence Road and Sharon Lane as the site for a future church. The group asked to use the site, and won approval.

*The "Brown Building," first home of Providence UMC*

On May 16, 1954, by vote of the membership a name was adopted for the new congregation: Providence Methodist Church.

By September 1954 plans for the first church building had been drawn up, bids received and a fund drive was underway. The structure was to include a meeting hall with seating for about 300 worshippers, nine classrooms, an office and kitchen. Known as the Brown Building, it was ready for its first worship service January 9, 1955. It would serve the new church for more than a decade. A separate Children's Building was completed in 1959.

Sunday, July 18, 1965, was a red letter day for Providence Church. On that day the cornerstone was laid for the impressive brick sanctuary which stands today. Nine hundred forty-five persons attended as Bishop Earl Hunt delivered the sermon. In 1996 the Brown Building was demolished to make way for the latest phase of construction, which was completed in 1998. It includes a chapel, classroom, recreational and multipurpose facilities for all ages. A columbarium has since been added. In spring 2002 a bronze bell was installed, a gift of Mr. and Mrs. Sam Powell in honor and memory of charter members of Providence Church

The original membership roster of Providence UMC lists 185 charter members. At the end of 2002 there were 2195 members and 424 baptized children and youth who had not yet made a profession of faith. Average attendance at worship was 781.

# Purcell UMC

Purcell United Methodist Church could say it was born in a motorcycle shop. Their first service was held October 13, 1946 at the Shaw Motorcycle and Supply Company at Wilkinson Boulevard and Camp Greene Street.

World War II had recently ended when a small group of westside residents first met at the home of Sam Goode. With help from the District Mission Society they began planning for a new church. Originally it was called "Camp Greene Methodist." (Camp Greene was a

*Purcell United Methodist Church*

massive World War I army training camp in the area where Purcell was established.) Before long, however, a permanent name was chosen: Purcell Methodist, honoring Bishop Clare Purcell. Early in their planning the congregation adopted a motto, "The little church with a big heart."

A site at Greenland and Weylan was selected for a new building. The Rev. J. J. Powell, their first pastor, later remarked he had been "appointed to a briar patch." Ground was broken November 28, 1946 on the first phase of the building project, a structure to be used as a fellowship hall. The building went up quickly, and by March of the following year it was ready to house a Palm Sunday service.

The next phase in construction was a sanctuary. The choir from Big Spring Methodist provided special music for the first service in the new building September 11, 1949. In 1963 a newer sanctuary was built.

# St. Andrews

In the fall of 1958 a group of people began meeting at various homes in the Montclaire neighborhood, and sometimes at Mouzon

Methodist Church. They would become the nucleus of a new congregation to be known as St. Andrews Methodist. The Rev. Glenn Lackey, executive secretary of the Charlotte District Mission Society, led in the organizing effort.

The Mission Society had previously purchased a five and one-half acre site on Emerywood Drive, and soon construction was underway on the first unit of a future church complex.

The first service was held in the building in April 1959, even before a full-time pastor was appointed. Two months later the church did get its pastor, the Rev. William H. Butler. By the end of the year, 172 members were on the church roll.

The following year a Women's Society was organized with three circles, as well as a Methodist Men's group. As soon as a kitchen was finished, according to the church history, the women began preparing suppers for the men's group. A weekday kindergarten was started with some 30 five-year-old youngsters.

By the end of the church's second year, membership had grown

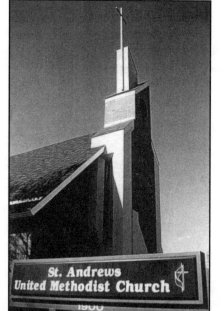

to 238 members. On Easter Sunday, 1963, the number stood at 442.

In 1965 work began on a new sanctuary, with an unusual twist. In making plans for the project, church members decided to build two churches at the same time, the other one being in India. In 1966 the new Charlotte sanctuary was consecrated.

Over the years additional renovations have been made to St. Andrews buildings, and its programs and missions have made steady progress. Membership now exceeds 900 persons.

# St. Francis UMC

Among the younger congregations in Charlotte is that of St. Francis United Methodist Church on McKee Road. The church was organized May 7, 1989, through the combined efforts of members from Myers Park, Providence, St. Stephen and Pineville United Methodist Churches. Their first building was completed in February 1994, and a Pavilion was added behind the first building in September 2002.

Providing affordable housing has been a focus of outreach at St. Francis. Together with St. Stephen, the church has participated in building a Habitat for Humanity house. Habitat was the theme for the church's Vacation Bible School in summer 2004. The youth group traveled to Kentucky and rural North Carolina to perform service work, and, as this went to press, the church was planning to send two building teams to Jamaica to help refurbish a church.

Enjoying healthy growth since its founding, St. Francis has a youthful, energetic congregation with average attendance in 2004 of more than 300 persons.

# St. John's UMC

In March 1934 Charlotte was coping with the Great Depression. The Oakhurst neighborhood, at that time on the outskirts of Charlotte, was a long ride from the nearest church, and residents longed for a place of worship closer to home.

From the beginning, members of the Waddell family have been prominent in the history of St. John's. Three of them, Mrs. R. B. "Granny" Waddell, "Mama Jo" Waddell, and her husband, J. R. Waddell, were instrumental in getting the future church organized. With help from the Charlotte Christian Men's Club and the Rev. J. A. Baird, a prayer service was scheduled in a private home. Soon thereafter an outdoor Sunday School class began meeting, leading to a revival the following year conducted by the Rev. Baird. In August

1935, they began assembling for worship in a rock building formerly used as a store, at the present site of H & S Lumber Company on Monroe Road. They organized themselves as a nondenominational congregation, choosing the name Oakhurst Mission. The charter membership consisted of five families, numbering 14 persons in all. They started a regular Sunday School, supervised by a Mr. Clontz.

In March 1937 the growing fellowship purchased the rock store building and adopted the name Oakhurst Interdenominational Church. A Women's Auxiliary had already been organized. Now a youth group was added, and an arbor, which they called the "tabernacle," was constructed behind the rock store to accommodate the increasing membership. At first the tabernacle had no sides and only sawdust for a floor, but many uplifting services were held in it. Later, the tabernacle was enclosed for use as a sanctuary and classroom building. A vestibule and steeple were added. The original rock building was torn down in 1938, and two years later a Sunday School addition was built.

Eight years after that first prayer meeting, the congregation voted in the summer of 1942 to affiliate with the Methodist Church, taking

*Above, left: The former rock store building and "tabernacle" which housed worship services for the Oakhurst Mission. Lower right: The tabernacle, with walls, vestibule and steeple added, home of the Oakhurst Interdenominational Church. The Interdenominational Church became St. John's UMC in 1942.*

the name of St. John's. Charter membership was 70 persons. Within a year membership had more than tripled and plans were being made for a new house of worship.

The Western North Carolina Conference pledged $25,000 and eventually another $6,000 was realized from the sale of the old church property. Altogether, the new building represented an investment of $75,000. The new sanctuary, one block east of the original church, was dedicated in June 1949.

By 1954, another expansion was needed, and work began on the J. R. Waddell Fellowship Hall. It was dedicated on Easter Sunday, 1966.

An interesting sidelight to the story is how the church gained an extra 50 feet of street frontage at its new site. In marking the property line for the fellowship hall, surveyors found a 50-foot wide strip of land adjoining the church property for which no ownership could be documented. Two members, Harry Davis and Ed Waddell, arranged to have the land deeded to the church for a much needed parking area.

In 1994 St. John's was recognized as a "Church of Excellence" in the Western North Carolina Conference, based on its activities in Sunday School, mission involvement, stewardship, youth ministry and evangelism. Over the years St. John's has made countless contributions to its community and to the city. One of the more noteworthy was founding Adult Care and Share, a day care facility for senior citizens. The center was moved to Cokesbury United Methodist Church in 1995 and continues to be a blessing to families struggling to care for aging members.

St. John's has gone from a simple neighborhood prayer meeting on the outskirts of Charlotte to a mature church in the midst of urban change. Surrounded today by a mixture of single family homes, apartments and businesses, it faces new challenges. But its congregation continues with optimism and courage as they seek to adapt to an uncertain world while focusing on the needs of church members and the community.

# St. Luke UMC

St. Luke UMC, founded in 1953, was the tenth in a series of churches started by the District Mission Society. The congregation first began meeting in homes, and later at the Methodist Home. At one of those early meetings at the retirement center, 63 persons were in attendance. But of those, 50 were residents of the Methodist Home; only 13 were potential church members.

The church's first minister was the Rev. Joe Warner, for whom this was his first appointment. The young pastor and his wife, Carolyn, rented a duplex, where some of the first members were baptized. The pastor's study was in his bedroom.

It was Rev. Warner's job to build the church from scratch. Soon after his appointment, he recalls attending a meeting of preachers and church school superintendents, at which each minister was asked to stand and introduce his superintendent. Rev. Warner, not yet having members or staff, had brought his wife, Carolyn. He introduced her, saying he was the only Methodist minister who could carry his entire congregation with him wherever he went.

When the church purchased the site for its sanctuary it was in a newly developing neighborhood, barely inside the city limits. Much of the work on the building was done by the members themselves, beginning after their regular jobs each day and working until midnight or later.

In August 1954 the new building was completed. By this time membership had increased to 100.

The church enjoyed a period of steady growth in the following years, attracting many young families. By 1968 the Sunday School had 136 children under the age of ten years. There were 20 classes for all ages, including five for adults. The church sponsored Boy and Girl Scout troops, four Cub Scout dens, a Webelos group, Brownies and Junior Girl Scouts. There was an active youth fellowship and a weekday kindergarten.

Members have been active in mission projects, including many who have served on building teams. For a number of years the church

*St. Luke United Methodist Church*

shared its facilities with a Native American congregation, which eventually found a new home.

Like many, if not most older churches, St. Luke faced a decline in membership in the 1990s and for a time considered merging with another Methodist church. But then, with a new minister and a renewed spirit, the church regained its momentum and maintains an active program.

# St. Mark's UMC

St. Mark's is one of a handful of churches in Charlotte which have made a successful transition in membership amid neighborhoods of rapidly changing character.

Once an all-white church, St. Marks was organized in 1959 in the Clanton Park area midway between Uptown and Charlotte Douglas International Airport. The church began with 88 members, drawn largely from the Clanton Park, Rollingwood and Edgebrook communities. But soon after it began, changing neighborhood patterns led the church to re-examine its mission. Today the church serves an all-black congregation, with an emphasis on meeting the needs of its community. It operates a child day care center and focuses, as well, on senior citizens.

The church sanctuary was erected in 1978.

*St. Paul United Methodist Church*

# St. Paul UMC

St. Paul United Methodist Church was organized in 1948 and completed its original building, at 2830 Dorchester Place in the Sedgefield neighborhood, the following year. A new sanctuary was constructed next to the older building in 1957.

As with many of today's churches, St. Paul has been challenged to maintain its membership, but thanks to the generosity of members past and present it has maintained an active, mission-oriented program. It participates annually in the Carolina Cross Connection, involving youth and adults who spend a week at Pfeiffer University in Stanly County. They go out each day to perform volunteer yard work and home repairs for needy residents of nearby counties. Another program at St. Paul, "Faith, Hope and Love," provides after-school mentoring and Bible study to at-risk youngsters from area schools. Volunteers from St. Paul also help provide meals at the Winter Shelter.

# St. Stephen UMC

On June 10, 1968, Bishop Earl G. Hunt, Jr., appointed the Rev. Jim Armstrong to start a new church in southeast Charlotte. Before the month was out, Rev. Armstrong had held an organizational meeting at the Charlotte Athletic Club. A month after that, a name for the new church was selected: St. Stephen.

The first worship service was held September 8 at Lansdowne Elementary School, and the same evening 69 persons became charter members of the new congregation. Progress continued at a breathless pace. A church school was begun almost immediately. The United Methodist Youth Fellowship was launched on September 22, a Women's Society was organized on October 8, and the Men's Club met for the first time October 13.

The congregation met at Lansdowne School for six months, then accepted an invitation to use a former sanctuary at Sardis Presbyterian Church. Within a year the church more than tripled its size, to 229 members.

A site for the future sanctuary at 6800 Sardis Road had been purchased by the Charlotte District Mission Society in December 1968, and ground was broken for the new building in April 1971. Before the ceremony, colored stones were buried at the site, to be dug up and given to members as keepsakes of the event. The stones symbolized the stoning of St. Stephen, the first Christian martyr, for whom the church is named.

The new sanctuary was consecrated March 5, 1972. By this time nearly 400 persons were on the church roll. Since completion of the original structure, St. Stephen has added a gym and more classroom space.

# Sharon UMC

Sharon United Methodist Church was officially organized October 2, 1966, but its beginning goes back to 1961. In September of that year the Charlotte District Mission Society bought a six acre plot on Sharon Road near Fairview. Had other plans not intervened, Sharon Church might today be sitting on land that is now occupied by the Dillard's Department Store in SouthPark! But nothing was built right away, and about four years after the purchase, the previous owner offered a swap—a bigger site across the road, seven and one half acres in all. It is the site where Sharon Church sits today. The exchange also netted the future church $60,000 in cash to go toward construction.

At the Annual Conference in June 1966 the Rev. John McWhorter was appointed to lead in forming the new church. Within a month a parsonage had been acquired, and in another month interested families had begin meeting at the parsonage with Rev. McWhorter. On September 4 Bishop Earl G. Hunt preached the first sermon to the new congregation at Sharon School.

The following Sunday produced one of those events that are always remembered in church tradition. When members arrived at the school for morning worship, there had been a janitorial mix-up and the building was locked. In fine old Methodist tradition, the service–their first-ever morning service–was held outdoors, in the shade of a giant oak tree. According to an article in the next day's *Charlotte Observer*, Mecklenburg County Fire Commissioner Michael Allen was present, and arranged to borrow some folding chairs from the Sharon Volunteer Fire Department for the worshippers to sit in.

By November the church had its first officers: Frank Finley, lay leader; Will Buchanan, board chairman; Dwight Phillips, chairman of the Building Committee; Mike Allen, Church School superintendent; and Bill Cook, treasurer.

Even before their own building went up, the congregation plunged into mission work, giving $2,500 to help erect a new church

*Sharon United Methodist Church*

in Pakistan. They also provided support to a Vietnamese child, and provided funds and volunteers for a host of Charlotte-area agencies.

After a successful fundraising campaign, ground was broken for the church building March 2, 1969. It was completed and occupied on July 19, 1970. The building was enlarged in 1980, with wings for Sunday School and the Wesley Center added later.

Today the church continues to serve its community by supporting programs such as Bethlehem Center, Crisis Assistance Ministry, Habitat for Humanity, the Uptown Day Shelter, Room In The Inn, and Loaves and Fishes.

# Simpson-Gillespie UMC

Simpson-Gillespie United Methodist Church can rightfully claim historic status on several counts.

For its roots we look back nearly a century and a half to the end of the Civil War, and newly-freed slaves seeking to build their own institutions. Their church, established in 1866, was named Simpson Chapel Methodist Episcopal Church. The first meeting place was in the shade of a birch arbor in the 300 block of South Graham Street. William Davidson, Isaac Adams and James M. Goode were among those early worshippers.

*Simpson-Gillespie's first church*

The church was formally organized the following year, and named Simpson Memorial Methodist Episcopal Church, after Bishop Matthew Simpson. Membership grew rapidly, as the population around it also increased.

In 1957 the church moved to West Trade Street, taking over a building formerly used by Wesley Heights Presbyterian Church.

An even bigger move came 11 years later, when the all-black Simpson Methodist voted to merge with Gillespie Methodist, a white church. It was a bold move, especially considering the racial climate in the mid 60s. They became Simpson-Gillespie, combining the names of the two former churches as well as their congregations. The merger service September 2, 1969, was well-attended by both black and white members.

Today members worship in an inviting building they occupied in 1988, located at 3545 Beatties Ford Road. It is a far cry from that first open-air worship service under a tree 138 years ago.

# South Tryon Community UMC

Originally called "South Tryon Mission," this new Charlotte congregation was launched as a joint venture of Myers Park UMC and the Charlotte District. It was begun in 2001, and is located at 2516 South Tryon Street. Among programs offered by the church are a fellowship luncheon on Tuesdays and Thursdays, and a "Sidewalk Sunday School" on Wednesday evenings.

# Spencer Memorial UMC

It was a full century ago, 1904, when Spencer Memorial Church was organized in a north Charlotte cottage. The house, owned by Highland Park Manufacturing Company, served as the church's home for three years. Originally known as Highland Park Methodist, it became North Charlotte when the congregation moved into its first permanent building on North Caldwell Street in 1907. The church changed names again in 1913, becoming Spencer Memorial, in memory of J. S. Spencer of Highland Park Manufacturing, who had provided significant help to the church in its early years.

In 1942 the church exchanged its Caldwell Street property for its present location on 36th Street. The property was occupied by an old YMCA building, which was remodelled to provide a temporary sanctuary and classrooms. But it was nearly two decades before the new sanctuary was built. The first worship in the new building was held July 23, 1961. A new educational building was added in 1982.

# Thrift UMC

Thrift Methodist Church was begun in 1914, when the Rev. Benjamin Franklin Fincher was appointed to a charge consisting of Moore's Chapel, Big Spring and Thrift. Big Spring had been orga-

*Thrift Methodist Church, built in 1915-16; destroyed by fire in 1938*

nized at least as far back as 1866. Moore's Chapel dated from 1884.
Thrift was brand new.

The congregation first met in an upstairs room over the old Sadler
store building in Paw Creek. Money was scarce on those days. Minutes from the first quarterly conference in 1915 show the church raised
$6.10 for the preacher.

Work began in that year on the church's first building, with the
minister and members contributing much of the labor. The cornerstone was placed by Bishop John Kilgo on July 25, 1916. The first
parsonage was built in 1918.

J. K. Beatty was a charter member of the Thrift congregation,
and was a leading member for many years. He is shown as recording
secretary for the first quarterly conference. Later he served as the
first Sunday School superintendent. When the Sunday School began, it had four teachers and 54 "scholars." The first collection was
$1.96. Others on the first list of stewards were T. W. Ingle, W. L.
Howe, R. E. Holder, R. H. Sells, and D. P. Randall.

The picturesque old wooden structure was destroyed by fire in
1938, and was replaced by the brick building which is still in use

today. Ironically, the first service held in the new building was the funeral for J. K. Beatty.

The Rev. E. M. Graham was appointed the first full-time pastor at Thrift when it became a station charge in 1945. In 1958, under the pastorate of the Rev. Tom Stockton, a new educational wing was completed. Additional property, including the Kendall Community House, was purchased in 1962.

As with most Methodist churches, the women of Thrift deserve special mention. The Women's Missionary Society was started by Mrs. J. W. Little, who had studied to be a missionary, and joined the church in 1928. Over the years the women have spearheaded numerous projects in service to the community and the world. Their bazaars have financed many improvements to the church itself.

# Trinity UMC

Trinity United Methodist Church goes back to 1814, when it began as a "preaching place" in the home of Margaret Kerr Martin. Earliest records of the fellowship simply refer to it as "Martins," following the custom of naming congregations for the homes where they met. As the little society grew, they organized a church known first as Buckhill, and later as Trinity. A more detailed history of Trinity Church is provided in a previous chapter.

# University City UMC

Although University City is a relatively new church, its roots go back more than a century to the founding of Belmont Park Methodist Episcopal Church South in 1897. Belmont Park opened its doors at the corner of Harriett (now 15th) and Pegram Streets in the brand new Belmont Springs neighborhood, which took its name from springs in a nearby park along Little Sugar Creek. The first minister was the Rev. J. A. Baldwin, who had been headmaster of Southern Industrial Institute, a Methodist institution in the Hoskins community. Over time a number of Charlotte firefighters and their families joined Belmont Park, and it became known as "the firemen's church." The church grew rapidly, and by 1940 members began planning to build a new facility. They chose a site on Hawthorne Lane, but the new building would not be completed until 1953. The first service there was held on Easter Sunday.

Unfortunately, the church soon found its neighborhood in transition, and faced the prospect of declining membership as longtime residents moved away. Congregational leaders realized another move was necessary if the church was to survive. Most members agreed.

In 1985 the Charlotte District began exploring plans for a new church in the University City area of northeast Charlotte. The Rev. Dayle Groh, pastor of Belmont Park, took part in the discussions. He proposed the idea of using the people and resources of Belmont Park as the core of the new church, but it would be another year before the plan was accepted by the district.

After much waiting and negotiating, a site was finally acquired at Harris Boulevard and Cheshire Road.

On February 28, 1988, members of Belmont Park voted to dissolve their church and dedicate all its financial resources, property and the core of its congregation to form the new church. A New Mission Development Committee was organized to make plans. The new church held its first service April 18, 1988, at Mallard Creek Elementary School. The choir and many members of Belmont Park took part in the 9 a.m. service, then rushed back to Hawthorne Lane for the 11 a.m. service at Belmont Park.

One question was a name for the new church. In one late-night meeting a committee member jokingly suggested, because of the church's proximity to Charlotte Motor Speedway, the new church be called "Speedway to Heaven UMC." They could build a large tower and paint it in black and white checks with a large arrow pointing to Heaven. A motto was also suggested: "Get out of the pits, come join us." "University City" proved to be a more down-to-earth choice.

The new name was formally adopted on June 19, 1988, when a Constituting Conference was held to officially launch the new church. District Superintendent Harold Wright delivered the morning message. Charter members were received; one infant and three adults were baptized; and five others were accepted on profession of faith. The new church was on its way.

More than two and one half years would pass before University City would get its permanent home. After many delays and much anxious waiting, on February 17, 1991, the new building at Harris and Cheshire was close enough to completion to be used for its first service. Perhaps a portent of future success: Attendance at the last service in Mallard Creek School was 257 people; at the first service in the new building, attendance was 576. In 2004 the membership was more than 2200.

# Vermillion Community Church

One of Mecklenburg's newest congregations is the Vermillion Community Church in Huntersville. The church has an unusual history. Vermillion is a residential development near downtown Huntersville—one of those currently popular new projects that recreates the look and feel of an old-time neighborhood, with tree-lined streets and a business area designed to look like a village square. In a move that is not common, but in keeping with the overall "feel" of the neighborhood, the developer set aside land for a church, and approached the Western North Carolina Conference for help in starting a congregation.

The conference accepted and tapped the Rev. Karen Easter, then an associate pastor at Davidson UMC, to organize the new congregation. Easter brought an unusual background to the new assignment. Professionally, her background was city planning. She had been deputy director of the Historic Preservation Division in the Georgia Department of Natural Resources. The ministry was a second career.

She began work at Vermillion in the fall of 2001. The congregation now numbers about 90 persons. They currently meet in the Community Room of the NorthCross Medical Center on Statesville Road in Huntersville. Within the next two years they hope to begin work on their church building.

# Wesley UMC

In the summer of 1976 the Charlotte District Mission Society concluded, after a neighborhood survey, a new church was needed in the Candlewyck/Olde Providence area of southern Mecklenburg County. Within months a pastor, Buddy Champion, had been appointed to lay the groundwork for the new congregation. On February 13, 21 persons attended a planning session and a week later the first worship was held at the Olde Providence School library. The church was officially chartered April 10, 1977. Work continued during the year, and when the charter enrollment period was closed in December, 109 persons were on the roll.

In 1978 ground was broken for Wesley's first building, at 3715 Rea Road. The second phase of the building plan, a new Sunday School and child development building, was completed in 1996.

# Zoar UMC

"Zoar" is a Biblical word that refers to a special place of refuge. Records of the old Sugar Creek Circuit show "Zoar" as a preaching place as early as 1815. However, that Zoar, in Iredell County, was not connected with the Zoar United Methodist Church which exists today near the York County line in southwestern Mecklenburg County. The present church traces its founding to prayer services organized by J. P. Blackwelder and held in a brush arbor at the home of Hamilton Smith on Youngblood Road in 1861. Originally, this congregation was part of the Methodist Protestant denomination, which had divided from the Methodist Episcopal Church in 1830. Methodist Protestant and Methodist Episcopal churches were reunited in 1939.

The growing congregation erected their first permanent building, a log cabin, about a mile from the church's present location. They moved again to the site of the present church, on a tract donated by Billy Smith. In 1901 a newer building replaced the first on the same site.

In 1955, members, contributing their own labor, began construction of the present building, which was dedicated in December of the following year.

An acre of land for the adjoining cemetery had been given many years earlier by Sam Wilson, whose son Lewis Wilson later donated another half acre. In 1944, Thomas Adkins and Olin Krimminger donated additional land for the cemetery.

The Christian Education Building was completed in 1967.

At various times in its history Zoar has been affiliated with several annual conferences, including the South Carolina Conference. In June 1969 Zoar became a permanent part of the Western North Carolina Conference.

# Bibliography

Abbott, F. C. *50 Years In Charlotte Real Estate*. Privately published, undated.

Alexander, J. B., M.D. *The History of Mecklenburg County from 1740 to 1900*. Charlotte: Observer Printing House, 1902.

Alexander, J. B. *Reminisces of the Past Sixty Years*. Charlotte: Ray Printing Company, 1908.

Andrews, Mildred Gwin. *Myers Park United Methodist Church, 50th Anniversary*. Charlotte: Myers Park United Methodist Church, 1975.

Betts, Albert Deems. *History of South Carolina Methodism*. Columbia: The Advocate Press, 1952.

Billingsley, A. S. *Life of the Reverend George Whitefield*. Philadelphia: P. W. Zeigler and Company, 1878.

Blythe, LeGette and Charles R. Brockmann. *Hornets' Nest*. Charlotte: McNally of Charlotte for the Public Library of Charlotte and Mecklenburg County, 1961.

*The Book of Discipline of the United Methodist Church*. Nashville: The United Methodist Publishing House, 2000.

Borio, Gene. "Tobacco Timeline—A Fascinating Journey." Article published on the Tobacco BBS WebPage, 1997.

Carroll, Grady L. E., editor. *Francis Asbury in North Carolina*. Nashville: Parthenon Press.

Claiborne, Jack. "Ivey Overcame Weak Eyesight With Merchandising Foresight." *The Charlotte Observer*, May 5, 1990, p. 14A.

Clark, Elmer T. *Methodism in Western North Carolina*. Nashville: Parthenon Press, 1966.

Clark, Elmer T., editor in chief. *The Journal and Letters of Francis Asbury*. 3 volumes. London: Epworth Press, 1958.

Clay, James W. and Douglas M. Orr, Jr., editors. *Metrolina Atlas.* Chapel Hill: University of North Carolina Press, 1972.

Chreitzberg, A. A. *Early Methodism in the Carolinas.* Nashville: Publishing House of the Methodist Episcopal Church, South, 1897.

Davidson, Chalmers G. *The Plantation World Around Davidson.* Davidson: Briarpatch Press, 1982.

Davis, Sarah I. *Covenant Made on Earth, A History of the Louisburg United Methodist Church.* Chapel Hill: The Chapel Hill Press, 2001.

Dooley, George W. and Jerome C. Huneycutt. *A Century of Service—A Story of Calvary Methodist Church.* Charlotte: Privately published, 1965.

*The Duke Endowment—Questions and Answers 2000.* Charlotte: The Duke Endowment, 2000.

Foote, William Henry. *Sketches of North Carolina.* New York: Robert Carter, 1846.

Gerdes, Phillip E., editor. *Historical Sketch of St. Mark's Evagelical Lutheran Church.* Charlotte: privately published, 2000.

Grissom, W. L. *History of Methodism in North Carolina.* Nashville: Publishing House of the ME Church, South, 1905.

Hastings, Charlotte Ivy, editor. *Our Mecklenburg Heritage.* Charlotte: Privately published by the Children of the American Revolution, 1955.

Hood, Dellmann O. *The Tunis Hood Family: His Lineage and Traditions.* Portland, Oregon: Metropolitan Press, 1960.

Hutchinson, Orion N. *A History of Harrison United Methodist Church 1785-1955.* Unpublished manuscript, 1955.

Ivey, Joseph Benjamin. *My Memoirs.* Greensboro: Piedmont Press, 1941.

James, Marquis. *The Life of Andrew Jackson.* New York: The Bobbs-Merrill Co., 1938.

Jenkins, James. *Experience, Labours and Sufferings of Rev. James Jenkins of the South Carolina Conference.* Privately published, 1842.

Kerr, Russell Martin. *The Presbyterian Gathering on Clear Creek.* Charlotte: Jostens, 2001.

King, Victor C. *Lives and Times of the 27 Signers of the Mecklenburg Declaration of Independence of May 20, 1775.* Charlotte: Anderson Press, 1956.

King, William E. "Washington Duke." Essay published on the Duke University Website, 1995.

Kratt, Mary Norton. *Charlotte: Spirit of the New South.* Tulsa, Oklahoma: Continental Heritage Press, 1980.

Kratt, Mary Norton and Thomas W. Hanchett. *Legacy: The Myers Park Story* (Second Edition). Charlotte: Myers Park Foundation, 1990.

Leard, Samuel. "Methodism in Anson County." *The Southern Christian Advocate*, July 17-August 21, 1846.

Lee, Jesse. *A Short History of the Methodists In The United States of America Beginning In 1766, And Continued Till 1809.* Baltimore: Magill and Clime, 1810.

Maynor, Joe. *Duke Power, The First 75 Years.* Charlotte: Delmar, 1979.

McEwen, Mildred Morse. *First United Methodist Church.* Charlotte: Heritage Printers, Inc., 1983.

McNitt, V. V. *Chain of Error.* Palmer, Massachusetts: Hampden Hills Press, 1960.

Moore, M. H. *Sketches of the Pioneers of Methodism in North Carolina and Virginia.* Nashville: Southern Methodist Publishing House, 1884. Reprinted by Attic Press, Greenwood, S. C., 1977.

Parker, Percy Livingston, editor. *The Journal of John Wesley.* Chicago: Moody Press, 1951.

Pettus, Louise and Nancy Crockett. *The Waxhaws.* Rock Hill: Regal Graphics, 1993.

Ray, Worth S. *The Mecklenburg Signers and Their Neighbors.* Austin, Texas: Self-Published, 1946.

Robinson, Blackwell P. *The Five Royal Governors of North Carolina, 1729-1775.* Raleigh: The Carolina Charter Tercentenary Commission, 1963.

Saunders, William L., editor. *Colonial Records of North Carolina,* Vol. 7. Raleigh. 1886.

Sauer, Charles A. *A Pocket Story of John Wesley.* Nashville: Discipleship Resources, 2002.

Telford, John. *The Life of John Wesley.* London: Epworth Press, 1947.

Tompkins, Daniel A. *History of Mecklenburg County and the City of Charlotte,* Vol. I. Charlotte: Charlotte Observer Printing House, 1903.

Walser, Richard. *North Carolina Legends.* Raleigh: North Carolina Department of Cultural Resources, Division of Archives and History, 1980.

Wesley, John. *Journal.* London: J. M. Dent & Sons, Ltd., 1913.

Wheeler, John H. *Historical Sketches of North Carolina From 1584* to 1851. Philadelphia: Lippincott, Grambo & Co., 1851; Reprinted in New York by Clearfield Co., Inc., 1925.

Wheeler, John H. *Remininisces and Memoirs of North Carolina and Eminent North Carolinians.* Columbus, Ohio: Columbus Print Works, 1884.

Woodmason, Charles. *The Carolina Backcountry on the Eve of the Revolution.* Chapel Hill: University of North Carolina Press, 1953.

**184**

# Index